The Star Mountains Expedition to Dutch New Guinea in 1959

Personal experiences and impressions

B.O. van Zanten

The Star Mountains Expedition to Dutch New Guinea in 1959

Personal experiences and impressions

Uitgeverij Aspekt

The Star Mountains Expedition to Dutch New Guinea in 1959
Personal experiences and impressions
As translated by Alice McCreary
© 2017 B.O. Van Zanten
© 2017 Aspekt Publishers
Aspekt Publishers | Amersfoortsestraat 27
3769 AD Soesterberg | The Netherlands
info@uitgeverijaspekt.nl | www.uitgeverijaspekt.nl
Coverdesign: Mark Heuveling
Lay-out: Paul Timmerman

ISBN: 978-94-6338-210-6
NUR: 680

Disclaimer – The author and the publisher have made every feasible effort to determine and acquire copyright permissions for material presented in this book. If any right-holders have been overlooked we kindly request them to apply the publisher.

*To my parents (†) who made it possible for me to study biology
and in turn take part in this expedition*

Preface

The Star Mountains expedition to the central range of Dutch New Guinea was the last big scientific expedition to a mostly unknown area. As a member of this expedition, it was my job to collect mosses, lichens, and fungi.

Sadly, I did not keep a diary during the expedition, and so to try and reconstruct my experiences after at least fifty years is a big task. I am mainly able to reproduce most of my experiences due to my memory of many of the events. Though the dates of these events have often slipped my mind, these can be reconstructed by use of the data I collected, as all materials were supplied with a date, location and any other particularities. I was able to refer back to this data through my publication *Mosses of the Star Mountains Expedition* (1964) about the lichens I collected on this expedition. The story about the journey to the top of the Antares is, however, mainly based on notes I made upon returning to basecamp. I am also grateful for being able to use the diary of Brongersma, the scientific leader of the expedition, as many of the events that I remember are also mentioned in his diary with the dates. I managed to gain information more from the letters that I sent home, and from the book about the expedition *Het Witte Hart van Nieuw-Guinea* by Brongersma & Venema (1960). What was also useful were a variety of newspaper articles, written by myself and by others, which contained a lot of information about our experiences. The most important sources I used to refresh my memory were, however, the hundreds of slides and black and white photos which I took whilst there.

In this rather belated diary, I only give my personal adventures, experiences, and impressions. The things I was told by others are only mentioned if they directly influenced or had something to do with my own experiences. Therefore, this diary in no way has the pretension of being a complete narrative of the expedition. It does, however, give a rather full report of my own experiences and, because of this, acts as a good supplement to the afore mentioned book by Brongersma & Venema. In their book there is, for example, nothing mentioned about my wanderings between the fourth of May and the twentieth of June when I was not at the basecamp in Sibil.

With regards to most of the higher plants I saw while on the expedition I often only knew the family names or nothing at all. Of the higher plants which caught my eye, I made slides. Based on this, upon return to Holland, Cees Kalkman (the higher plant man on our expedition), Prof. Dr. W.G.G.N. van Steenis (Leiden) and others were able to tell me most of the species names, or at least the genus or family names. For this I would like to thank them.

Ben van Zanten, to the left in 1959 and to the right in 2013

Becoming a bryologist and participating in the expedition

My interest in plants has been a part of my life since I was a young boy and was further stimulated by my father, who seemed to know all the plants in the area we lived when I was young. We lived in Oudemolen, a farmers village in the North of Drenthe, where my father was head of the local public primary school. I can remember that my father owned the first edition, from 1900, of *Heukels' Flora van Nederland* (Heukels' Flora of Holland) and that when I turned ten I received my own copy, the eleventh edition from 1934. From that moment, this book was so frequently used it lived on our kitchen table ready for both myself and my father.

My oldest brother Jan had left for the Dutch East Indies before the war, and often wrote to us about his experiences, but also about the plants and animals he saw, even sending a dried specimen of a plant he found. As a captain in the Koninklijk Nederlands Indische Leger (Royal Dutch Indian Army) he was captured by the Japanese as a prisoner of war in Thailand. He survived, and upon his release at the end of the war immediately started sending me more dried plant specimens and letters Singapore.

For me there was never a doubt that after my HBS time (old Dutch equivalent of GSCE's) in Assen I would start studying biology in 1950. During the course of studying biology in Groningen, the lectures by Ms. Dr. Ch.H. Andreas made a great impression on me, due to her descriptions of many kinds of exotic plants, and her slide shows which showed herbarium material as well as pictures.

During the first part of my studies in Groningen, I was taught a lot about tropical vegetation by Prof. Dr. R. van der Wijk. He often told me of his experiences during his first Indonesian expedition to West-Java and Sumatra in 1952. As he was specialised in mosses, he had collected many moss samples on his travels to Indonesia and has asked Wim Margadant, who worked with us in the botanical laboratory for the Index Muscorum, to help sort and name what he had collected. Additionally, we had received a collection of Indonesian mosses which had been collected in 1949 and 1950 in West-Java by two Indonesian collectors, Noerta and Soekar. We also had two collections of mosses as collected by Wim Meijer from 1952, and 1954 from West-Java and Sumatra. All of these collections and specimens had to be determined, something which Wim Margadant could obviously not do alone. At this point I had become a student assistant to Professor Van der Wijk, who asked me to help Wim with his determinations. I had not yet had any experience with regards to the determination of moss sorts, especially not tropical species. But Wim quickly and expertly taught me what the main tropical families and genera were. After this, through the constant coaching of Wim I gained a lot of experience with regards to determining tropical mosses. It may seem strange that at this time I felt more at home with Indonesian mosses than with Dutch mosses, but nonetheless I was very interested to see all of these mosses I had helped categorise in their natural habitat.

The Koninklijk Nederlands Aardrijkskundig Genootschao (KNAG), the Maatschappij voor Natuurkundig Onderzoek in East and West India and the Rijksherbarium in Leiden had made a plan at the start of the fifties to set up a big multidisciplinary expedition to the last, practically unknown part of the central range of Dutch New Guinea, the Star Mountains, close the border of Australian New Guinea (now Papua-New Guinea). Its highest peak, the Antares is about 4000 metres high. The organisers of the expedition thought it would be fruitful to send along a researcher who was specialised in, and would focus on, the collection of the lower plants. With previous expeditions there were very few mosses or lichens collected, as there was not a specialist. Anything that had been collected was mainly the bigger specimens which the higher plant researchers brought with them (Zanten 2003).

In about 1958 Prof. van der Wijk asked Prof. H.J. Lam, director of the Rijksherbarium in Leiden, if he knew someone who had enough experience with tropical mosses and would not be afraid of the heavy physical exertions under primitive conditions in the rainforest. The first choice fell to W.D. Margadant (Wim). He was, however, previously engaged, as he had been hired by ZWO (Zuiver Wetenschappelijk Onderzoek) with a special subsidy to compose the Index Muscorum. As this could not be put on hold, there was no way for him to join the expedition, meaning that I was the only person in the Netherlands qualified for the job. Naturally, there was no way that I could pass on the opportunity to personally study and explore the rainforest. There was, however, one problem, as I was in the process of writing my thesis about a family of tropical bryopsida musci frondosi (*Trachypodaceae*). This meant the thesis needed to be finished a lot earlier than I planned for, so I no longer had time to write a chapter about the relationships within and without the family, nor did I have time to add an index. My promotion took place on the third of March in 1959, leaving me with only a month to prepare for the expedition.

The preparation

Not knowing what to expect from the expedition meant that I also had no idea what to do with regards to preparation. Therefore, I went to Dr. W.G.N. van der Sleen, a geologist and specialist in beads from the seventeenth century, for advice. I had met Dr. W.G.N. van der Sleen during a trip with the KNNV (Koninklijk Nederlandse Natuurhistorische Vereniging) and knew that he had been to the tropics several times. He was able to give me some good advice, including two books about former expeditions of the KNAG Koninklijk Nederlands Aardrijkskundig Genootschap) to New Guinea, to prepare me for the local environment. These books were about the Southwest expedition to New Guinea in 1904/5 and the expedition of 1936 by A.H. Colijn. All participants were also given the standard work about the mountain Papuans of New Guinea by C.C.F.M. Leroux (*De berg-papoea's van Nieuw-Guinea en hun woongebied, 1948*) by publisher Brill in Leiden. I also started reading books about the jungle, written by Anthony van Kampen, through which I gained great insight as to what could be expected from the tropical rainforest.

Van der Sleen stressed that it was very easy to get lost in the rainforest and that you must never go exploring on your own. It was also important to clearly mark the path you were following by use of, for example, twigs, or cutting pieces of tree bark so that you could always find your way back. He also advised me to never go into the rainforest with short sleeves, because this would only invite small cuts which could then start to irritate and form sores. This was especially important towards the beginning of an expedition, as through time one would get used to the tropical sores and become somewhat immune. If you did, however, get any scrapes or cuts it was of upmost importance to treat them immediately with an iodine solution. Van der Sleen also told me that it was a good idea to always carry biscuits, or some other type of food because you could suddenly get hungry and find it nearly impossible to continue further. Bringing stock cubes was also a good idea due to the loss of salt from sweating. Another piece of useful advice was to always have sewing equipment and safety pins handy in case buttons came off or clothes got torn. As there would be no dentist on the trip it was also important to get a thorough check up before I left and to invest in some 'clove' oil to numb or cancel out the pain in case I did get toothache. Nagel can mean nail or clove in Dutch. I bought the clove oil, only to later find out that I had purchased actual nail oil to be used on feet or finger nails. Luckily I found this out in time, so I still had the opportunity to buy clove oil.

Furthermore, I was advised to bring, colourful, preferably shiny objects with me that could easily be stuck into things, like your hair, ears, or nose. These were to gift to the local people in the hope of becoming friends. For this I chose a bag full of ties for plastic bags, because they came in all different colours and glistened in the light.

Van der Sleen also advised me to take many pictures as we would be in an area where many unique images could be made, not only of the vegetation and the landscape, but also of the Papuans who, as far as we had heard, still lived in the Stone Ages. For this I bought two cameras, a Rolleycord and a Foderflex, both for 6 x 6 shooting. The first was meant for coloured slides and the latter for black and white photos. As the tropics are rather humid and moist it is possible that the celluloid layers of the film take up so much moisture they swell and stick together, making them practically unusable. To avoid this, I bought a special metal tropics casing for both cameras. I made a deal with Jos Lange, the owner of the photo shop where I bought all my equipment and rolls of film, that I would send all of my full film rolls back to him to get developed, and that he would let me know if something wasn't right. He did this at one point when my slides of the Papuans were underexposed. Because of the dark skin colour of the Papuans it was necessary to expose the slides containing Papuans for a longer time period. We also came to the agreement that if I was ever low on rolls of film I would send him a telegram and he would immediately send me more rolls. Jos Lange also advised me to bring proof of where I purchased my equipment with me so that upon return to the Netherlands customs would not think I bought them abroad and charge me for the import taxes.

Other than the useful information and advice I received from Van der Sleen, I also received a lot of information from Prof. Dr. H.J. Lam, director of the Rijksherbarium in Leiden. I travelled to Leiden several times, where he spoke about his own experiences in the jungle of New Guinea and shared other useful information, especially about the collection and treatment of the plant specimens I would find. Drying the mosses could be an issue. Air drying would be practically impossible due to the moisture in the air, meaning that I had to bring a dry-oven. I was able to borrow this from the Rijksherbarium. This was a light aluminium dry-oven with four hurricane lamps that ran on petroleum. The mosses could be dried in the dry-oven in paper bags, then as soon as they were properly dried they needed to be put in airtight plastic packaging. The Rijksherbarium was willing to provide me with the paper bags, storage boxes (cake boxes), plastic bags, labels and any other collection and shipping supplies I needed. They also printed field books in which I could note down the necessary data to match the collection numbers of the collected species. They also gave me field books for New Zealand as my plan was to travel there after my expedition to visit my brother Gerrit, who emigrated to New Zealand after his military duty ended in around 1951, and, I had not seen in almost ten years.

During one of my visits to Prof. H.J. Lam he showed me a black and white picture, which had only been taken recently, of the Sibil valley in which you could see the building of the base camp in progress, the recently constructed airstrip and the meandering Sibil river. In this picture you could also see that along the river there was bush like vegetation interspersed with what looked like cane fields. The picture also showed fenced gardens belonging to the inhabitants of the Sibil valley. Just behind the camp you could clearly see a doline (sinkhole) and spread along the river there were some bigger trees which Prof. H.J. Lam identified as being part of the *Albizzia* family.

Prof. Lam told me how he had always found the preparation for an expedition very exciting, but that during his expedition in New Guinea he often wished that he had never joined. This was because the daily tasks of wading through mud, with a lot of rain, heat, leeches, mosquitoes and the endless green ended up being rather depressing after a while. The many beautiful plants, and friendly Papuans, however, supposedly made the endurance somewhat worthwhile. He told me, that upon return to Holland the miserable tasks are quickly forgotten and the good memories are what you are left with. He also added to this that no expedition ever goes as it is planned, so a lot of patience and the ability to improvise is a prerequisite.

I also heard from Prof. Lam that other than the dry-oven and the field books for the expedition we would be provided with footwear, outerwear, a blanket and a mosquito net. The rest of our clothing was up to us to provide, and of course it was our own responsibility to get the right immunisations and enough malaria pills. Needless to say I always enjoyed my conversations with Prof. Lam.

Before our adventure began all of the expedition members within Holland got together in Leiden in order to meet, and get to know each other. The members were Wim Vervoort and John Staats (both zoologist), Cees van Heijningen (taxidermist), Herman Verstappen (geomorphologist), André de Wilde (physical anthropologist) and myself (botanist).

It was agreed that the results of our expedition would be published in the magazine *Nova Guinea*, Vol. 16, the last edition that the magazine would publish in 1964. All of the collected material would become property of the Rijksherbarium. We were allowed to make duplicates of the bryophytes (mosses) for the herbarium of Groningen. We agreed with the media that each participant would report their experiences to a different newspaper. The newspaper I was assigned to share my experiences with was 'Het Vrije Volk'. In order to sign my contract with them I had to go to their editorial office in Amsterdam for the day. On this same day I received my wages for doing so (about 200 guilder) and they took a picture to add to the article. Later on it turned out I had forgotten to report this wage to the tax people, meaning I was also told not to let them know what I did with this money. I had bought film rolls with it which was accepted, meaning the amount did not get added to my overall wages.

The Expedition

Saturday the 4th of April until Monday the 6th of April
Flying from Schiphol to Biak

On the fourth of April 1959, a Saturday morning, I took the train to Utrecht with my mother where in the afternoon we met up with Uncle Wout and Aunt Puck (my mother's sister and her husband) and continued our journey to Amsterdam. The bus that was supposed to take us from the Central Station of Amsterdam to Schiphol was full. However, the driver told us that we could take a taxi to the airport and charge this back to the company, so this is what we did. After checking in we drank coffee in the Schiphol restaurant, where we could see how my baggage was being loaded into our plane (the KLM-constellation Phoenix). In the restaurant we met up with the other expedition members leaving from Holland. This was all very exciting for me, not just because it was to be my first time on a plane, but also because we were travelling to such a far-away tropical destination.

We departed the airport exactly on time (18:45), just before it got dark. There were a great number of young men around the age of twenty in the plane, they were Marines dressed as civilians so as to avoid trouble on our change overs. After about an hour's flight we arrived in Frankfurt where we had half an hour to go to the restaurant. After this we boarded another plane to Rome. By this time it was completely dark so we were able to watch the lights of Frankfurt during our take off. At around midnight we arrived in Rome where we had a little longer to grab a drink in the restaurant. After which we continued our journey to Beirut in Lebanon. While flying across the Mediterranean Sea it started to get light so we could see Cyprus and the coast of Lebanon. Just after sunrise we landed at the airport in Beirut, which was on the coast due to mountains leaving little other space for it. Some of these mountain tops still had snow on them. It was at this airport that we first saw men wearing fezzes and veiled women, who wore a kind of black gauze covering their head. When we left this airport we first had to collect our passports, which we had previously had to hand in, from a big noticeboard. This, to me, did not seem very safe as it meant that anyone could take your passport. Luckily, I managed to find my passport soon enough and the next part of our journey started. For this we had to fly over the mountains, and in order to gain enough height first had to fly a circle over the sea.

The whole of Sunday (the fifth of April) was spent flying over the dessert areas of Syria, Jordan, Iraq and Iran in order to get to Karachi in Pakistan. During this whole flight there was not a cloud in the sky, however we were flying too high to be able to see any of the landscape. In the evening we arrived in Karachi which is located on the South coast of Pakistan. While at the airport I had some time to write a letter home to let them know how hot it was. We were taken from the airport to the KLM-hotel in the town in order to freshen up. The men in Pakistan had fine black beards, a turban on their head and wore a kind of dress, there were also cows on the street. In the night we left for Calcutta where we arrived on the morning of the sixth of April. Before we were allowed to get off the plane, the plane was disinfected, so we had to sit in the plane while they sprayed the contents of a spray can in the plane putting us in the smell and fumes. This did not seem very healthy to me. After this we weren't allowed to stay in the plane and our passports were taken again. In the meantime, the plane was thoroughly checked and cleaned. There was, however, time for some food. Here the men wore turbans as they did in Karachi. The airport was heavily guarded by soldiers, even when on the toilet there would be a man with a turban and a gun stood behind you. Our journey then continued to Bangkok in Thailand. On this part of the journey we saw the delta of the Irrawaddy River in Burma, nothing but forests sectioned off a great many anabranches of which the silty water which flowed into the sea could clearly be recognised. In Bangkok we were able to walk around in the area of the airport. I noticed that the more to the East we travelled the more ground stewardesses there were and the prettier they got. At this airport I managed to send a few more cards home. Then our journey continued to Manila in the Philippines where we arrived towards the end of the afternoon. We had to wait here for a while because a plane that was to fly over the North Pole to Manila was delayed, and several passengers from that plane needed to board our plane. Due to this we had some time to investigate the area the airport was situated in, which was at the edge of town. Just outside the fence there was a small shelter made of bamboo and reed where someone was selling fruits. The trading was done through the holes in the fence. We also walked into the town down a broad boulevard along the coast where there was a lot of traffic, especially jeepneys (jeeps left over from the war that have been built into taxis, decorated with catholic images and lots of music) and buses who were continuously honking their horn and playing loud music. It was like a fairground. We were constantly being stopped by taxi drivers who showed us pictures of naked women claiming that they could arrange anything for us, such as a 'closed room'. We also saw little houses that were stood on poles with reed and corrugated sheet roofs and welcoming toko's. It was here that we saw our first tropical plants along the side of the roads, though a lot of it was *Mimosa*. That same evening, we left for our final destination Biak where we were to arrive at half past three in the morning local time.

Tuesday the 7th of April
Biak, 'arrested', flight to Sentani.

The airport of Biak was located close to the kampong Mokmer and was also called Mokmer. It was an international airport belonging to the Dutch part of New Guinea and was on the south coast of the island Biak which was, in turn, located on the coast of New Guinea in the Geelvinkbaai (now Cenderawasih Bay). Under the guidance of a naval transport officer we travelled from Mokmer to the nearby naval airfield Boroekoe, where we were able to eat and shower in the recently built navy base. The same morning, we were supposed to be flown in a Martin Mariner belonging to the Dutch Royal Navy to Sentani, the airport of Hollandia (now Kota Baru). This dual motor plane is amphibious and so can land on water as well as on land. To be able to land on water there is a float fastened to both wings. The plane we were supposed to take was, however, not flight worthy therefore we had to wait for another plane to be made ready for take-off. The radar on the new plane didn't work properly either, however the pilots did not seem to mind this so much. Due to the delays we were only able to leave in the afternoon, so we still had time to go for a walk through kampong Mokmer. The kampong was small and as far as we could see consisted only of one broad street with trees, and houses with big front gardens on both sides. Because all of this was new to us, we were very interested and looked at everything. I can imagine that the inhabitants were not very happy with this. The new marine base and airport with several barracks were on the coast and we were invited here to have a meal in the wardroom. We were served by impeccably dressed Papuans and the window looked out over the sea and the clearly visible silhouette of the outstretched island of Japen.

Upon return to the airport Boroekoe I saw the Marine's Martin Mariner in which we would fly to Sentani. I thought that it would be nice to take a picture of the plane, but did not even stop to think about the fact that, it being a naval plane, taking pictures of it would be prohibited. There were a lot of people walking around in perfectly white clothes, which I found out later was the Navy's tropic uniform. It looked nothing like the military uniforms I was used to and I honestly thought they were civilian staff. When I tried to take a photo of the plane I was 'arrested', however after telling them that I was a member of the expedition, and them checking it with my colleagues I was released again. Because of this debacle I did not get the chance to take a picture of the plane, however I would have another opportunity to do this in Sentani.

The six of us were squeezed into the cargo space of the Mariner, which is actually a transport plane, and nearly cooked alive. The space was extremely small, probably about 4 square metres and about a metre and a half high, it was also extremely warm because the sun had been shining on the plane all day. Shortly after we took off one of the crew members was able to give us some fresh air by opening several small shutters. The motor of the plane made a horrendous noise, and to cheer us up one of the pilots told us about how the Mariner was not really a very trustworthy plane and that it sometimes happened that one of them would crash.

We were able to take turns to look outside through some small side windows. To start off with we were flying over sea but could clearly see Japen and after that the coast of New Guinea came in to sight. First we saw the stretches of swamp forests on the delta of the Mamberamo river, which Prof. Lam had already told me about. After this the coast became rocky, and we saw hills stretch out under us. The hills were covered in grass (*alang-alang*) and in the valleys some small streaks of secondary forests were visible. Within no time we saw the Cijcloop Mountains, these mountains are quite narrow and only around 60 kilometres long, but still reaches a height of 2000 metres, bordered in the South by the Sentani Lake. This lake is stretched out and whimsical in shape, as it is about 30 km long and rather narrow with many large coves, making it an unforgettable sight from the air. Along nearly all of the banks of the lake there were small stretches of trees. The Sentani Lake used to be part of the sea until it was closed off from it, in turn making it a fresh water lake in which sharks and sawfish, who gradually adapted to the fresh water, still swim.

At the airport there were several reporters and camera people waiting for us. Wim Vervoort, the leader of our group did the talking. A photographer took a picture of our group while we were stood in front of the Mariner and this picture made it into most of the newspapers in Holland.

I was now also able to take close up pictures of the Mariner, so it being prohibited in Biak was rather senseless. During this welcoming party Terco Simon Thomas was also present, an entomologist who I had already met at the Zoological laboratory in Haren. He told us how the provisioning of our base camp in the Sybil valley from Merauke was seriously delayed which meant that we may not be able to do much to start off with.

As soon as we arrived in Sentani, as in Biak, the first thing I noticed was the lovely herbal smell coming from the abundance of flowers and plants in combination with the high humidity.

Arrival in Sentani. From left to right: Staats, De Wilde, v. Heijningen, Verstappen, v. Zanten and Vervoort

We were taken to the Governments hotel in Hollandia-Binnen in a Volkswagen van where we would stay for several days. Terco Simon Thomas joined us, and on the way told us all about the different trees we saw on the journey. Sadly, this went rather quickly and due to this and the sheer amount of new impressions I am unable to remember much of it.

The hotel, which was situated on a small hill was simple but very convivial. The servers were mostly Papuans who were extremely polite and well dressed, but did not yet understand very much Dutch. When you asked them something, they nodded politely, but did nothing because they had no clue what you were trying to say. We had been warned about this already though. I, together with probably many other Dutch people, was under the impression that Papuans would be rather coarsely built and not very evolved. Upon actually meeting them however this proved not to be the case. The temperature was always above 30 degrees and hardly cooled down at night either, as was to be expected.

Originally the idea was that we would travel to the base camp in the Sibil Valley the next day in a Twin Pioneer. This was impossible because the plane was unable to fly, for reasons unknown to us. So instead we would have to spend at least two days in Hollandia-Binnen. We didn't really mind this, as it meant we were able to take the time to recover from the long journey and get used to the moist and humid heat.

Wednesday the 8th of April
Hollandia-Binnen, lots of sleep.

It had rained a lot the previous night, and during the day it also rained frequently. Just before we arrived here it had also rained a lot, and as often happened several landslides had taken place meaning that the road to Sentani was temporarily blocked. All of this was still visible during our bus journey to the hotel, even during our stay more landslides took place.

Because of the rain we were unable to do a lot, and in the hotel we were confronted with the news that in Hollandia-Haven it often rained even more. Being practically forced to do nothing was actually a welcome rest. I spent the whole day sleeping, and when it was twilight I did not know whether it was morning or evening, I sometimes wished people good morning when it was actually evening. People must have questioned our capabilities as scientists based on this behaviour. However, I quickly discovered that even when you were sleepy you were able to figure out whether it was morning or evening; in the morning there was always a bird singing in a very melodic way, in the evening there was not. After a couple of days I regained my sense of time and slowly started to get used to the heat and humidity. My brother, Jan had already warned me that upon arrival in the tropics the first few days would be spent feeling awfully sleepy.

Thursday the 9th of April
Going to Hollandia-Haven. Boat trip to Humboldt Bay. Walking back to Hollandia-Binnen. Gecko's. Van Sprang in our hotel.

Together with the biology group I took the Volkswagen van from the hotel to Hollandia-Haven where we planned on taking a boat trip in the governmental boat on the Humboldt Bay in the morning. There was also a theatre group with us on the boat who were performing that evening in Hollandia-Haven. Along the coast there were lots of fishermen's houses in the water stood on long posts. There were also several pirogues on the water. Across the beach there were several landing boats from the second world war rusting away, as this was the area where the Americans docked in 1945 in order to expel the Japanese. In the harbour you could even see the remnants of a rusting American war boat. We also saw a Martin Mariner land on the water and make its way to the coast. After our boat trip we walked back to Hollandia-Binnen, which was about six kilometres, so that we could look at the different plants and animals along the road. On the beach we saw a lot of *Ipomoea pes-caprae*, which had completely taken over a rusty landing boat so not much of the boat could be seen anymore. Though everything was still very damp from the rain of the previous day, the weather was beautiful and the sun was shining. There were no mosses to be found anywhere, but there were a lot of blooming higher plants. These were almost all plants that were unknown to me or plants I had only ever seen in pictures, for many of them I didn't even know which family they belonged to. The plant world was very much overwhelming, as there were so many different kinds with simply magnificent flowers. You could barely take a step or you would see something else which was even more pretty than the one before. I can remember that on the side of the road along the harbour I saw the passionflower (*Passiflora Foetida,* from America), a lovely red convolvulus like flower (*Cuamoclit* spec.) in the crack of a rock, we also saw a tree which had been *completely* taken over by another convolvulus which was in full flower (*Ipomoea* spec.), a fern (*Gleichenia* spec.), *Mussaenda* spec. (*Rubiaceau*) with its noticeable lightly coloured leaves and an orchid with light purple flowers (*Spathoglottis* spec.). For me, what was special was a 2-metre-high bush close to the water which was completely covered by a parasite (*Cassytha filiformis*). All of these plants made a big impression, even though I was unable to find a sing1le moss, which was my actual goal. I can also remember seeing a lot of *Mimosa invisa* (giant sensitive plant) on the roadside whose thorns could easily cut you if you were wearing short trousers. However, I had followed Van der Sleen's advice and was wearing long trousers.

On the road we saw several dead snakes who had been driven over by cars, apparently they were common in the alang-alang fields. Towards the evening it started to rain again and upon arrival at our hotel we discovered that there were gecko's everywhere, inside, as well as outside in search of insects and frequently making the 'tjitjak' noise. Of course these geckos had been there since before we arrived, however, until this point we had been too tired to notice them. At night, when I was already in bed I saw a gecko on the wall slowly creep towards a fly. When the gecko was about twenty centimeters away from the fly, the fly moved his wings but stayed where he was. The gecko jumped so much from the fly's sudden movement that he fell off of the wall, and the fly survived the attempted attack.

In our hotel the journalist and radio reporter Alfred van Sprang was also present. I did not know him, however Wim Vervoort, who had met him before, introduced him to our group and he told us how it was also his plan to travel to Sibil, in order to report on our expedition. I found him to be rather arrogant and did not pursue any contact with him other than saying good morning and good evening. It appeared that others from our group felt the same way about this.

Friday the 10th of April
Official start of the expedition. Hollandia-Binnen. Sending of first day envelopes with expedition stamps.

On this day the expedition was supposed to officially start, but we were still stuck in Hollandia and there was little to be done in Sibil because of the rain, at least that's what we were told by Brongersma (the scientific leader of the expedition) via the radio. We did leave the hotel early in the morning and travelled to Sentani in the hope that the Twin Pioneer would still fly to Sibil. But the night before there had been another landslide due to the rain, meaning that the road to Sibil was temporarily blocked. Even if we had managed to reach Sentani it wouldn't have helped as we were told that the Sibil valley was too overcast. In Hollandia-Binnen it had rained for a great deal of the day again, the only thing I was able to do was try and collect samples outside the hotel in the periods that the rain held up. This however was without results, as there was not a single moss to be found. The many walkers I saw on the roads did not seem to be bothered much by the rain, however they all used a banana leaf above their head as a kind of umbrella.

As there was a post office in a barrack like building close to the hotel I was able to send my first letters to Hilly, family, and friends, together with the nice bird of paradise stamps, and new expedition stamps. A young Papuan girl worked in the post office, and she stamped our letters very carefully with a stamp press with such a long handle I was surprised she always managed to hit the stamp. To honour the official start of the expedition people were able to purchase a first day cover for the Star Mountain stamp, of which I sent several to Holland.[1]

Saturday the 11th of April
The vain leave for Sibil.

Finally, we were going to leave for Sibil. It was good weather in Sentani, and in Sibil it had also refrained from raining the previous night,

---

[1] Later it turned out that there were no firs day covers available in Sibil. They made their own stamp with the text: 'FIRST DAY OF ISSUE STARMOUNTAIN. OK SIBIL. 10 APRIL. 1959'. Several envolopes were given this stamp on the 10th of April. I was however still able to get these envelopes with the same stamp labelled the 10th of April on the 14th of April. According to the stamping I sent a letter home from Sibil on the 10th of April, this would have been impossible as at this time I was still in Hollandia and I only arrived in Sibil on the 14th.

meaning that the airstrip was usable and everything seemed favourable for the flight. We left the hotel at 5 o' clock in the morning and travelled to Sentani. The mess from the landslide had been cleared up, so the road was free for us to drive. We were weighed before being allowed on the plane, as was our baggage. Our plane took off and quickly we were flying above the clouds. We were only able to catch glimpses of the rainforest every now and then through the clouds. However, the message reached us that the Orion mountains behind which the Sibil Valley is situated was too overcast for the Twin Pioneer to fly through. Meaning that there was no point in continuing our journey, and we were forced to turn around again and go back to Sentani and our hotel.

Sunday the 12th of April
Hollandia-Binnen. The first moss. Dojo. Agricultural Research Station.

As it was Sunday there was no plane planned. This left us free to do whatever we thought was fun and useful. Directly behind the hotel the alang-alang covered hills started, in which there were carved valleys with secondary forest remnants. This is where I collected my first moss sample, which was growing on a shadowed rock in a forest remnant. Just above this mossy rock there was a large spider web and a small spider with very long blue legs and white rings. When I got close the spider started shaking in an attempt to scare me off.

In the afternoon we (the biologist group) took a jeep to Dojo, a kampong situated at an altitude of 100 metres on the Northwest shore of the Sentani Lake and could be reached along a long gravel road. Along this road there were several houses in the alang-alang fields. One of these houses existed only of a floor with poles and a leaf roof, with a women squatting inside. When we passed the house on the way back, the woman was still sat in exactly the same position. The houses in the Kampong were built on poles and were situated on the edge of the lake in the water, the roofs were made out of reed and corrugated iron. The general transport used by the villagers, mostly fishermen, were pirogue's (hollowed out tree made into a canoe). Close to this kampong there was a river which came from the the Cycloop mountains which flowed into the Sentani lake. We took the jeep as far as we could across the riverbed, and then continued by foot across the pebbles in the water. This was a sweaty process due to the heat. One of the most remarkable plants along the river was the *Costus speciosus* which was in full flower, and a plant I knew from the Hortus in Groningen. John Staats was also able to shoot the first bird of his collection here.

On the way back to our hotel we visited an agricultural research station situated in Hollandia-Binnen. From the road not much could be seen other than a building, and through the windows you could see that they were growing plants. Other than this a rather inconspicuous sign stated that the station was here. We made our acquaintance with the staff, one of whom was Cees Verloop, someone who I did not yet know, but I would later do a lot of work with as he became a head of the gardeners of the botanical garden in Haren.

Monday the 13th of April
Hollandia-Binnen. Investigate alang-alang fields. Snakes. Termites.

The Twin that we were going to use to fly us to Sibil was needed to supply the famous Balliem Valley so once again we had the whole day to do whatever we wanted. In the afternoon I went back to explore the alang-alang fields and the fragments of secondary forests which were still present in the valleys around our hotel. We had been warned that there were a lot of snakes, and that to avoid these we should make lots of noise and wave a stick around so that they would flee. This is what I did, and I never saw a snake there. That they were very common to the area was no surprise as we had seen many dead snakes on the road on our way here. It was never clear to me whether there were also poisonous snakes in this area.

In the alang-alang fields themselves I was unable to find any mosses, but I did see some interesting higher plants. There were screwpines (*Pandanus*) scattered around, and I also saw a lot of *Melastomum polyanthus*. In many areas you could also clearly see how the top layer of soil was slipping away exposing the red soil common to the area of the Sentani Lake. This area also gave you a nice view of Hollandia-Binnen, and you were able to see the Humboldt Bay and the Sentani Lake from the hills. From the hills it became clear how between the alang-alang fields there was still quite a lot of remnants of the forest.

Close to the hotel, but more distanced to the road there were also indigenous houses on low poles with leaf roofs. This is where the Papuan servants who worked in the hotel lived. In one of the forest remnants of a valley I was able to collect two moss species. Because of the heat and the humidity plant material rots very quickly, meaning that mosses hardly get the time to prosper in the substrate. This meant that up until this point I had only been able to collect about five different species of moss, not a lot at all, but there was simply nothing more to be found.

Along the side of the roads there was a lot of *luecaena glauca* (mimosa), the grass (*Pennisetum purpureum*) and on a ruderal area there was a magnificent yellow-flowering *Cassia alata*. Close to our hotel, but also in other areas there were trees which contained big termite nests. These nests could grow to be half a metre or more and where pushed up against the sides of the tree trunks. From the bottom of the nest there was always a small tunnel which was stuck to the tree trunk and allowed the termites to walk to and from their nest without being seen. In the gardens the *Hibiscus* (Malvaceae) was most common. The hibiscus flowers were often used as decoration in hair or above the ear, also by many men. The road to Sentani went through a piece of primary forest close to Hollandia-Binnen where along the road there were different tree sorts, the most noticeable one was the *Artocarpus* (breadfruit) and the *Philodendron* which was sometimes covered in a fig like species, the *Ficus*. In the direction of Sentani there was a good view of the Cyclone Mountains, of which the peaks were in the clouds.

Tuesday the 14th of April
Really going to Sibil. Culture shock.

This was the day that we finally managed to actually reach the Sibil Valley. In Hollandia the weather in the morning was bad with rain, but we received positive messages over the radio from Sibil. Because it had hardly rained in the night the airstrip had dried out enough and the skies were hardly overcast. In Tanah Merah, to the south of the central range and where our plane originated from it was also good weather. This meant that we would probably be able to fly, so we had to get up early, have breakfast at five in the morning and collect our baggage. The hotel's Volkswagen van brought us to Sentani again. However, for us, the expectation that this flight would actually happen was quite low as it was pouring with rain from low hanging grey clouds. At the airport we were all weighed again while the Twin Pioneer, which had already arrived from Tanah Merah was prepared for take-off.

At half past seven that morning there had been radio contact with Sibil and it appeared that the weather was still good there. The Twin was owned by a private airline of New Guinea the *Kroonduif*. This plane was perfect to use in this are as it only needed a short airstrip to land or take off. The landing strip in Sibilant was only 400 meters, but this was enough for the Twin Pioneer. Other than the six expedition members who had come straight from Holland the government physician, T. Romain, who lived in Ifar by the Sentani Lake, was also to join us.

After several minutes of flying we were encased in clouds and could, once again, only catch glimpses of the Sentani Lake. As soon as we were flying above the clouds we were able to look down on the majestic silver landscape of clouds. The cloud masses rolled into each other, and in some places it looked as if an invisible hand had pulled the clouds up into stiff peaks. Our plane went straight through these cloud masses and after a while we saw holes in the clouds through which we could see endless forests which was only interrupted by meandering rivers. The white sand in the curves of the river were especially noticeable, but in a lot of areas there were also oxbow lakes. I had the good fortune of seeing a group of bright white parrots who formed a clear contrast with the green of the rainforest. Here and there, especially along the wide parts of the meandering river areas could be seen where all the trees had been cut down.

In some places you could see fenced gardens, mostly in the meanders of the rivers. These gardens often still had dead trees. Later I was told that the reason for the dead trees is because it was too much work for the Papuans to cut down the bigger trees with their stone axes, so instead they lit a fire under the tree in order to kill it so that they would no longer be bothered by the shade. Though we saw these gardens we did not see any villages or houses.

The sights we saw quickly disappeared behind the clouds again. The closer we got to the central range the clearer the air became. During the flight we were allowed to take turns to sit in the cockpit in order to see a clear view of the rainforest below us and the mountains in front of us.

After about an hour of flying the mountain tops which divided North and South New Guinea loomed before us. This was the central mountain range with several high mountaintops reaching above the clouds. In front of us we could see the Juliana Mountains with its ice and snow-caps reaching about 4600 metres above sea level. To the left we could see the somewhat lower Star Mountains with Mt. Antares's highest top ranging about 4000 metres above sea level. This top was one of the most important goals of the expedition. When I saw the mountains I realised just how difficult it would be to climb them. This, however, did not scare me, rather it gave me the feeling of being challenged to master the mountain. I was very much looking forward to investigating and discovering the unknown, no matter how difficult the climb would be.

It did not take long before we were flying over the Orion Mountains. In order to do this the plane had to gain a height of about 4000 metres. Because the tops of the mountains were not covered in clouds we were able to go over smoothly, but on the other side of the mountain, in the Sibil Valley, there were clouds again. This made the pilots doubt whether we would be able to land or not. However, they managed to find a gap in the clouds through which the Sibil Valley could be seen and we were able to land.

As soon as we descended through the clouds we saw the strongly meandering Sibil River and next to it what looked like a small, insignificant line which we were getting close and closer too and was to be our airstrip. The plane made a sharp turn to the left and we were descending quickly. The line became a smooth lawn outlined by bright flowers that we later saw were yellow marigolds, which Van Kampen had already mentioned in previous books. We were now also able to see several barracks and our welcoming committee consisting of several white people and a lot of Papuans. At this point the plane was still travelling at a high speed as we shot past the trees. The plane bumped around a bit while the motors made noises as they decreased the speed, and quickly we were taxiing along the lawn to the people who were waiting for us.

These people were, as far as the members of our company were concerned, Sneep and Herbets (both government officials), Kalkman (higher plants), Anceaux (linguist), Pouwer (cultural anthropologist), Reynders (agroecologist), the marine doctor Tissing, several marines, and of course Brongersma (the leader of the expedition and zoologist). While we were all busy shaking hands, talking, smiling, and having our pictures taken our luggage was unloaded by several Papuans and taken to the camp. The plane quickly departed again so that it would not be stuck at our camp, as it could be seen that the mountains were to be covered in clouds any minute. After we made first acquaintances we went to our barracks.

At the entrance of the camp, probably to accentuate that we were entering a special area, a sign had been placed stating that passports must be kept at the ready. We received a blanket, shoes and some clothes and were shown to our sleeping areas in one of the barracks. The beds existed of two poles between which jute bags and a mosquito net had been hung. I was surprised that the camp was no way near finished. Several of the barracks were still being built, thankfully our sleeping places had been finished already.

I spent some time in the afternoon talking to other expedition members. Around six we received our first meal (rice) in the 'Zilveren Huis' (silver house), the headquarters of the camp. Because it had been a long day, and it was already dark at seven I retired to my new bed quite early. That first night I slept excellently, though I was sometimes woken up by the rain falling on the aluminium of our roof.

The arrival in Sibil was of course a complete culture shock. We had been warned about this when we were in Holland, so that we were somewhat prepared. However, the culture shock mainly existed due to the Papuans in their traditional Sibil dress. This mainly consisted of a penis sheath for the men, and small reed skirts for the women. The paint and decoration on the head, arms, and legs of the Papuans and the busy talking and gesticulating of especially the male Papuans only furthered this culture shock. Surprisingly enough it only took us a couple of days before we no longer noticed that we found ourselves in a very special area. Here people still lived in the Stone Age and the Papuans who lived here had never before come into contact with Western people before.

Wednesday the 15th of April
Lost photography supplies. Exploring the base camp and the area around the airstrip. Caterpillars are tasty.

After being informed as to where I could find my equipment it turned out that a lot of the necessary things had not yet been delivered. My drying-oven and paper bags I needed for my collected material to be dried and saved had not yet arrived, neither had part of my photography equipment. This meant that I couldn't actually do anything yet. The expedition had two helicopters to their disposal who were supposed to transport the necessary equipment from Tanah Merah, 150 kilometres away in the South, to our camp. But the helicopters had not yet arrived, and neither had their crew. From what I was told it appeared that the crew was still stuck in Tanah Merah. Both helicopters were unable to fly due to heavy clouds, defects, and sickness of the pilots. Even if the helicopters had been able to fly it would not have helped with regards to my photography equipment as no one seemed to know where it had gone. The equipment had been sent from Amsterdam, but I was told that it had not yet arrived in Biak, Sentani, or Tanah Merah. I only had one camera with a separate exposure metre with me. But the several film rolls I had brought myself had already mostly been used in Hollandia. A second camera (for black and white pictures), a tripod, macro filters and more film rolls would be sent from Tanah Merah. I could go into the field already, but collecting samples didn't make much sense. At this point I did not much mind this as, as far as I knew we would spend a long time in Sibil, and the equipment would be arriving any minute. There was so much to see and explore that I was not bored for a minute.

The Base Camp
(Called Sibil for convenience).

I spent most of the day exploring the camp and the area surrounding it. The base camp (called Mabilabol by the Sibilians) was situated by the southern slope of the Orion Mountain at the height of about 1300 metres on a flat piece of loamy soil on a terrace of the broad Sibil Valley. The camp consisted of several barracks and was situated about 100 metres away from the airstrip and 20 metres higher. The most important barrack was called the *Zilveren Huis* because the roof and the walls were made of aluminium sheets. The windows did not contain any glass. This is where the leaders of the expedition, Brongersma and Venema lived, Venema not having yet arrived as he was also still stuck in Tanah Merah. The Zilveren Huis also contained a room for the doctors Tissing (marine doctor), and Romeijn (expedition doctor), as well as a sick room, a room for the Marine, Lieutenant Nicolas, a sleeping area for the helicopter crew and a communal mess hall. The idea was that after we finished our expedition the Silver House would become the governmental post and so was set up quite luxuriously. Behind the Silver House there was a *mandi*-area (shower area) and several toilets. In the mandi-area there was a drum full of water and several cans so that you could throw the water over yourself. The toilets consisted of a deep hole in the ground. Of the other barracks only the ceiling was aluminium and the side and back walls were created with sail. The front was mostly open, and the floor was made of compacted clay mixed with small stones from the river which created an artificial boulder clay. I recognised these kinds of floors from the farms where I grew up, making me feel at home quite quickly. It was in these barracks that the participants of the expedition lived. The scientists, technicians, and marines all had their own barrack. Because the temperature was still quite low at night a 'heater' had been placed in our barrack. This was made out of an oil drum in which a wood fire could be made. In emergencies it would be possible to dry plants above this fire. There was also a barrack which had been set up as a kind of laboratory. In the middle of this barrack there were several tables and chairs at which we could work. Just in front of the marines' barrack there was a flag pole with the Dutch flag, which often did not move because of the windless weather. There was also another barrack which was situated lower down in which our supplies were to be kept. A lot of work had been done in order to create electricity. Just in front of this barrack a landing area had been created for the helicopters. The whole of the camp had been built in close proximity to where the original governmental post had been situated, as I was told by the government official Jan Sneep when I visited him. This governmental post was a primitive hut that had been built up of corrugated sheets and sail, and is where Jan Sneep and Herberts, his predecessor, were housed. In this hut there were also two radio transmission and reception equipment, one for contact with the planes and helicopters, and one for radio contact.

By the camp there were also quite a lot of, about 25-metre-high, *Araucaria's* and several banana trees. Under the *Araucaria's* the floor was scattered with cones, some green and some which were starting to turn brown. Everywhere I looked in the vicinity of the camp I saw men and boys taking stones out of the Sibil and bringing them to the camp in order to create a pavement within and without the camp. All in all, the camp seemed, under the circumstances, rather comfortable and I figured that I would be able to survive here quite happily several months.

During my exploration of the camp I heard Cees Kalkman talking about the fact that two weeks ago he had walked from Mindiptana to the Sibil. It had taken him about two and a half weeks to walk the 150-kilometre route and that he had found this a very interesting journey. He had been dealing with intestinal problems throughout the whole of his trek, making it hard. He also told me that on the way, while still in the low-lands he had seen a banana tree whose bunches grew straight up in the air.

The Airstrip

According to Jan Sneep the airstrip in the Sibil Valley had been created about a year ago. It was quite an accomplishment considering the little equipment they had to their disposal. To turn a peaty area full of reed into a properly draining lawn is not an easy task to accomplish. Jan Sneep also told us how this had been done. It was very much due to the help of the Sibillers, who had carried a great amount of rocks from the riverbed to the strip. These rocks where then used as the base for the lawn. Just as important as the carrying of these rocks was the way in which the Sibilers helped to combat a caterpillar invasion which threatened the development of the lawn. When this happened Simon Terco Thomas (the entomologist in Hollandia) was asked for help, however, as soon as he arrived in Sibil the problem had already been resolved. The Papuans had discovered that caterpillars were rather tasty and so proceeded to eat every last one of them. The airstrip and path to the camp were surrounded by yellow marigolds.

Next to the path to the airstrip and the platform for the helicopters a place had been made for weather observations.

Thursday the 16th of April
Exploring the area around the base camp. Two friends.

I explored the area around the base camp. Close to the strongly meandering Sibil River there was reed like vegetation with a swampy underground. Jan Sneep told me how the river could sometimes overflow and that the area with the reed would then quickly disappear under water. This was also the reason why there were no trees growing in this area. One of the most noticeable plants along the river was the grass which stood almost as tall as a man *Coix lacrima-jobi* (Job's Tears). In other areas there were large gravel and sand plains. A little bit further away from the river, and slightly higher there were terraces with peat and loam. These terraces were primarily made up of woods with here and there areas of 1.5-2.5-metre-high shrub vegetation. One of the more common shrubs (*Eugenia*) had lovely red leaves. The most common trees were the *Araucaria cunninghamii* which were on camp territory, and *Nothofagus* spec.. The first type was able to grow very tall and normally had a very straight trunk. The *Nothofagus* was a lot less tall. The terraces retained rainwater for a long time in countless puddles. In some areas there were even clear signs of peat formation. This was clearly the case in a swampy area between the river and the camp. I was unable to find any special mosses on the peat ground, the kinds I found here later turned out to also grow in higher areas where they were better evolved. I presume that the frequent rainwater which flooded the peaty area prohibited the proper growth of these mosses. On the stagnating water of a small pool I saw, to my surprise a yellow flowering bladderwort (*Utricularia spec.*). The terraces turned out to be overflowing with different kinds of herb like plants, especially a lot of ground orchids. A noticeable plant was the *Hoya speciose* which had largely taken over a bush. Some other bushes had been taken over by pitcher plants (*Nepenthes Spec.*), a bladderwort as well as a flesh eating plant. This area was also rich with mosses, later on I would frequently revisit to collect mosses. At this point there was no point however as I was unable to dry the mosses.

In several places the rainforest reached up to the river. A bit further away from the camp to the East there were fenced gardens that I had already seen from the plane. Kalkman told me that in these gardens sweet potatoes (*Ipomoea Batatas*) and a grass specie (*Setaria palmifolia*) of which the young roots were eaten, were grown. Just behind the camp there was a lake, a doline (sinkhole) this was no surprise as we were in an area with limestone and karst topography. The existence of dolines was already clear to me as I had seen them in the aerial photos which Prof. Lam had once shown me. The edge of this doline was covered with several ferns. To my surprise the fern that we knew from Holland was also present, the eagle fern or common bracken (*Pteridium aquilinum*).

Another noticeable plant by the doline was the *Rhododendron konori* with its big, white, fragrant flowers. In the water of the doline there were two rather small ducks swimming. Close to our camp I discovered a very romantically situated log cabin with a garden where vegetables were being grown, this is where two American Protestant missionaries lived.

During my wanderings in the area around the camp there were two Papuan boys of about 7 or 8 who followed me around. They very much wanted to carry everything and talked non-stop. I, of course, did not understand a word that they were saying. I simply continued speaking Dutch to them and we pretended to understand each other. Sign language can do miracles in this kind of situation. They seemed to like joining me so much that they were with me throughout nearly all my time in Sibil. At one point one of them even slept under my bed in the camp. In doing so, he no longer had to walk home, and did not risk being late the next morning. I presume that they were from the closely situated kampong Kigonmedib or Koekding.

Friday the 17th of April
Going to Betabib.

My two friends arrived early and I thought it would be nice to go with them to the closely situated kampong Betabib. I had heard quite a lot about this kampong from within the camp and I was eager to check it out myself. The kampong was about two kilometres to the northwest of our base camp. A path led to it which was well trodden as the villagers often visited the base camp. The path went through open bushes full of flowering plants, of which a lot were ground orchids. Because of the frequent rain there were puddles everywhere, meaning that it was impossible to keep our feet dry, however today the sun was shining. After walking for about half an hour, we saw the houses. This was to be my first visit to a kampong whose residents still lived in the Stone Age.

The kampong consisted of a central area around which a one-metre-high wickerwork fence of twigs had been built. On the outside of this framework several houses had been built up against it. On the side of the square every house had small openings through which men were able to go in and out, on the outside there was a big opening through which the women entered. This opening was a lot bigger because the women had to enter the houses with a big bundle of firewood on their back. All of the houses were stood on poles of about half a metre high. The roofs were made of leaves which had been covered in twigs for stability. There wasn't a chimney because the smoke dissipated through the roof by itself. In the middle of the square there was a larger house. Around this house there was a messy looking veranda of about a metre high. The door was on the same level as the veranda and was shut off with a plank and some poles so that no one could look through it. Against this house there was a collection of planks and twigs in case something needed repairing. This bigger house on the square was the *iwool* (manhouse) and no women were allowed to enter it. Close to one of the houses and the fence around the square there was a group of Cordyline trees which were used as a medium between the villagers and their Gods. If the leaves turned yellow this was a sign that the Gods were unhappy about the villagers and meant that the villagers must evaluate what they could be doing wrong.

When we arrived at the kampong we were welcomed by two older, bearded men who were sat on the ground in the square. Both men were bald, which would have increased their respect within the kampong. We already knew each other because both men frequently visited our base camp. The one with the nice black beard was Bomdogi, landlord of the whole area including where our camp was situated. The other man, Wasonim, had a long grey beard. He wore a beautiful necklace of pigs teeth, a sign of his worthiness as governor of the iwool. They invited us to take a look inside one of the houses. When inside there was nothing to be seen other than a hearth.

Throughout my visit in Betabib I especially noticed how friendly and welcoming these people from the Stone Age were.

Saturday the 18th of April
Further exploration of the area around the basecamp.

Once again I explored the area around the basecamp with my two friends. Because of the great amount of mosses, I was continuously able to collect something new. My two friends slowly became so caught up in the collection of mosses that they became able to notice small differences in the mosses. Due to this, they often showed up with interesting findings, meaning that I no longer had to 'secretly' throw their material away. The big problem remained on how to dry the samples.

Sunday the 19th of April
The colouring red of the Digoel Mountains. To the vanishing point of the Sibil River. First meeting with the real rainforest.

In the morning, when everyone was still asleep we were woken by the voice of a marine who notified us that if we wanted to see something beautiful, we should get out of bed before it was too late. Because most of us had not woken up properly, nobody seemed to get out of bed. The voice repeated that it really was worth getting out of bed for. This is when I, and others realised that it really was worth getting out of bed to see what was going on- the sky was without a cloud which didn't happen very often. What we saw happen then in front of us was indeed unique. The rising sun was shining on the Digoel Mountains which coloured them a beautiful red. As the sun rose higher the red slowly faded until after about fifteen minutes the mountains had their normal grey-blue colour again. I was very grateful that the marine had woken us for this sight.

Like most days we went to the river in the morning to wash ourselves and our clothes. Herberts, the government official in the Sibil also joined us this time. When we were sat next to each other on a tree trunk we had a pleasurable conversation. He told me how it was usual to find the life of the Sibils quite normal after a couple of days, but he warned me that I should still make records of everything, and to keep proper photographic evidence, because it was so special to have the opportunity to experience the lives of people still in the Stone Age for a long period of time.

It was the first sunny day without any noteworthy rainfall. We took this opportunity to travel to the point where the Sibil River disappears in the ground. Wehad heard that about two kilometres to the East the river plunged into a deep hole, and this was something we were very interested to see. We went to the vanishing point with the biologist group, accompanied by several Papuan boys. In and around the river there were large sand and gravel plains and along the shore there were broad reed beds and peaty areas, but in other areas the rainforest reached right up to the river. The rainforest which we had to pass through every now and then became more and more impenetrable as we got closer the the hole. The river streamed into an increasingly narrow and steep ravine. Here the riverbed existed of big jagged rocks of limestone over which the water flowed as a gushing waterfall from terrace to terrace. We were able to follow the river over the terraces for a while until suddenly a towering cliff met us. In the meantime, the Sibil had changed from a casually flowing brook to a violent river due to the narrowing riverbed. With thunderous noise and big sprays of water the river rushed farther down, invisible to the eye into the rock and continued under ground. Later geologists worked out that the river travels underwater for quite a long time until it resurfaces again and goes on to the Ok Tsjop (East Digoel). We weren't the first to make this journey, as there had already been a path cut out through the rainforest. This was the first time I was to enter a real rainforest. What we had seen in Hollandia was as far as I know, all secondary forest. What I noticed was that everything was either green or brown, and that there were hardly any flowers to give colour to the whole. The ground was very muddy and there were dead slimy tree trunks everywhere. I had also prepared myself that there would be leeches, but I didn't see any. The area we were in was probably too high up and thus too cold. Though this was only a short journey, it was quite tiring because we were not trained, or used to walking over the rivers pebbles or the slimy tree trunks and mud in the rainforest. Later on, much harder journeys would not form an issue for us anymore.

Because of frequent floods, and probably human influence it appeared to me that the parts of the rainforest were not very well developed. In some places the stones along the river were nicely green with moss, (mostly *Pseudosymblepharis subduriuscula*) both the living and dead trees had mosses as well, but still there was less to be seen than I had expected. In areas where you could see horizontal branches over the water it was clear that the water could reach much higher as they were covered in dead plant remnants and silt had accumulated on them. That the river reached higher for longer periods of time was demonstrated by a moss (*Racopilum spectabile*) that richly grew on the overhanging twigs. On the normally developed parts of this moss there were offshoots with leaves that were smaller, lighter and spread more widely than was normal for this species. These are typical features of plants which have spent some time growing underwater. Along the shores in the open areas we also came across larger trees (*Albizzia*) which were grouped together. These are the trees which Prof. Lam had already recognised from the aerial photos. In the more shadowed areas we often found a busy lizzie with big white flowers (*Impatiens platypetela*).

Jan Sneep and Brongersma later told us that just before we arrived at the basecamp the Sibil river had risen due to the amount of rain in the Digoel Mountains. This lead the Sibil river to change from a peacefully streaming river to a violent mud stream. The water had been so high that even the airstrip had been underwater. The Papuans were not surprised about this flooding, as to make the airstrip higher stones from the river had been used, and according to them water was simply supposed to flow over these stones. To the Papuans the flooding was nothing more than the anger of the river. They warned us that the base camp was also at risk, as here stones from the river had also been used.

As it was such nice weather I went against the advice given to me by Van der Sleen and wore a short pair of trousers. It was, of course, unavoidable to not get caught on something and cut yourself in this area, and this is what happened to me. Because this happened often enough in Holland and never caused any problems I did not pay any attention to the scrapes I received. However, here in the tropics it is quite easy for a small scratch to turn into something very different, as I would later find out.

Another group consisting of Brongersma, Anceaux, Reynders, Romeijn, Vervoort and De Wilde, also utilised the good weather to take a trip to kampong Toeloe, which was situated on the other side of the Sibil River on a high terrace.

Monday the 20th of April
Going to the kampong Koekding.

On one of the following days, probably the 20th of April the biologist group travelled to kampong Koekding. This kampong was about eight kilometres north-east from the basecamp at about 1400 metres above sea level. We left early in the morning with five Papuan boys (of which two were my friends) as our guides and carriers. The first part of the path went through bush close to the camp, but this quickly turned into rainforest with rather steep parts. The path, which was in most places not much wider than half a metre was mostly made up of mud puddles, in which we sometimes sank up to our knees, rotten tree trunks, and fallen trees. Towards the beginning we attempted to keep our feet dry by jumping from one piece of grass or root to the next. This went quite well for some time, but at one point or another somebody made the wrong jump meaning they either landed in a mud pool or on a rotten tree in which they sunk. After a while everyone had wet feet. After this experience we decided instead to copy the Papuans and no longer bothered about trying to keep our feet, or anything else dry, this also turned out to be less tiring. In different places we had to wade through small streams and pass ravines. These ravines were mostly about 10 metres wide and 5 to 10 metres deep. At the bottom there was a small stream and the walls were rather steep and completely impassable due to the higgledy-piggledy tree trunks between which vines with sharp thorns hung. In order to pass these ravines several tree trunks had been laid across them, normally one or two big trunks, but sometimes also several thin trunks. These thinner trunks were often able to carry the

Papuans but not always the heavier Europeans. While crossing these there was often questionable creaking going on under our feet, but everything seemed to go well. The trunks were always slippery, even more so because of their frequent use. Because of these reasons the Papuans usually let us go first. Balancing on the tree trunks was often quite difficult. At one point, when I was in the middle of a slippery tree trunk going over a ravine I slipped, but I immediately felt myself being held so I would not fall. When I looked around I looked straight at the smiling face of one of our Papuan guides. His small feet strongly gripped on to the tree and he stood unswerving above the ravine. In one hand he was balancing the big package on top of his head and with the other he was holding on to me in order to stop me from falling. Our guides were true artists of the rainforest and seemed to feel it an honorary duty to ensure that we travelled through it safely. At every point of the path which was slightly harder to get through one of the boys was ready to give us directions on where we should put our feet in order to be as stable as possible. When we had all passed a difficult piece he would run to the front again in order to lead us over the next hurdle, for example a rotting tree trunk. These were often overgrown with moss, vines and ferns so that they were almost unnoticeable in the twilight of the rainforest. If you were to stand on them, it would be possible to sink down at least a metre deep.

In the rainforest a kind of stinging nettle grew which stung more viciously than any stinging nettle in Holland. It had the ability to inflict pain for several days on end. If there were only a couple of stinging nettles the guides carefully removed them. However, if there were too many the guides stood by them to warn us.

During one of our breaks one of our guides took a bone, a shoulder blade of some sort of mammal and a rotting tree trunk and started to take this apart. He ended up pulling several big beetle larvae out, which he showed us pridefully and shouted 'jaaap, jaaap'. We already knew this word and it meant something like 'nice' or 'pretty'. After this he bit off the hard jaws of the larvae and ate the rest.

After about two hours of toiling, sweating, and slipping our guides started shouting by making a sort of rolling noise with their tongue.

We would often hear this noise in the future, and it was used to warn kampongs that there was a group of people entering with peaceful intentions. Just after this the kampong Koekding came into sight. The kampong, which was situated on a hill, consisted of several groups of houses spread across about 200 metres. The houses were much the same as in Betabib, built along the outskirts of round squares. The squares were surrounded by a low fence of stacked twigs. The houses themselves were also round in shape, the whole of which was built on a floor of tree trunks situated about half a metre above the floor. On the part of the house that was turned towards the square there was an opening at about chest height. This door was only for the men, who basically had to climb through it. The other side of the house had a much larger opening which started the same height as the veranda. This opening was for the men and women. In one area a fence had been made and our guides made clear to us that we were not allowed to go over it. They shouted something like 'ajou piel' which we took to mean 'no entrance'. Behind the fence there was a big round area with an iwool in the middle, a sacred house for men which was forbidden to women. The square was also forbidden for women, unless there was a dance, in which case they were allowed on, but they were not allowed to enter through the gate. All of this information is what we later learned from the anthropologists.

One of our guides invited us to take a look in his house. We were allowed through the front entrance because we were real men. When we were all inside, our host (probably the father of our tour guide) threw some sweet potatoes on the fire to bake in honour of our visit. There was not much to see in the space, as there was no decoration or furniture. In the middle there was a hearth with above it a kind of platter on which tobacco and other things could be dried. When the sweet potatoes were finished we were asked to sit around the hearth on the floor. Our host gave us all a potato which he simply pulled out of the fire with his bare hands. Of course this was still very hot, and we had to be careful not to burn our fingers. We had to keep passing the potato from hand to hand until it had cooled down enough to hold normally and eat. It tasted quite good, like potatoes which have been frozen, but they were quite dry. In order to have enough protein, the people often ate insects like caterpillars and beetle larvae which they fish out of tree trunks, as we had seen earlier. Luckily we were not offered any insects. After we had finished our sweet potatoes we thanked our host and said goodbye with the knuckle greeting-process of entwining the fingers of one hand with that of the other person, and having the knuckles touch.

During our visit in the kampong we had noticed that there weren't any women. These were often kept in the background by the men, and also worked in their gardens and made sure there was fire wood. In order to travel back to our camp, we took the same route. On our way we came across several women who were heavily laden with fire wood and it became very much clear to us why the back entrances of the houses had to be so big. We were safely brought back to our base camp by our guides, after which they walked back to Koekding to spend the night there and were present again the next morning to help carry stones and guide us around the area outside the camp.

This excursion had made quite an impression on us all, it was a further acquaintance with the rainforest and the visit to the kampong gave us an experience of what the life of people in the Stone Age was really like. What we especially noticed was the friendliness and helpfulness of the Sibil's. It was a very positive experience.

Anceaux, Pouwer and De Wilde had gone to Kigonmedib with a couple of Papuan police officers. This Kampong was on the other side of the Sibil. The idea was that they would spend four days there to study the language, and that De Wilde would take physical measurements of the inhabitants.

Tuesday the 21st of April
Still on mandatory rest at the base camp. Lack of ballpoints. Thunder.

The idea was that the Twin Pioneer would come from Tanah Merah with the rest of our equipment. We would then also be able to give our post to the Twin, the first time it arrived in the base camp. I was busy writing because of this, and had also written down my impression of our journey to kampong Koekding and the vanishing point of the Sibil River for *het Vrije Volk*. I had also written down the story that I had heard from Simon Terco Thomas when I was in Biak for *het Vrije Volk*. Before I started writing I only had one ballpoint left that still worked, the rest had not yet been delivered and were probably in Tanah Merah. I wrote to Hilly to ask whether she could send me some extra fillings. I also had issues sticking my letters shut, with the resin from the *Araucaria's* it seemed to work well enough but still it wasn't a great success.

It is interesting what I wrote home about the expedition: "Since the 15th of April there hasn't been a plane. The equipment needed to dry the specimens (dry-oven, paper, packaging material etc.) has not yet arrived and the necessary clothing and shoes are only partially complete. Nobody knows when this will be coming, so the only thing we can do is wait. A large portion of my photography equipment, like my second camera, extra films, lenses, tripod, has also not yet arrived. All of this was sent from Amsterdam but did not arrive in Biak, nobody knows where it is or what happened to it. From a scientific outlook it may have been better to stay in Holland for an extra month. Though I do not have the equipment I need for drying and keeping the samples of my collected mosses I am having a tremendous time in Sibil. There was so much to see, both regarding the Sibil inhabitants and the plants, that I am never bored. We have several months left, and then my equipment will have arrived.

In general, the temperature is rather pleasant ranging from 20-25 degrees in the afternoon. It does rain often, but most of this happened at night meaning we weren't bothered by it. Today, however, towards the end of the afternoon dark clouds came over the Digoel Mountains making the Sibil Valley look quite threatening. With one of my last film rolls I was able to take some pictures of it. The thunder didn't take very long, but it did continue to heavily rain after this. At night this rain continued and the monotonous clatter could be heard on the aluminium roof of our barrack."

Wednesday the 22nd of April
Base camp. Group Herberts left to explore the area of the Ok Tsjop. Twin flies over with our stuff from Tanah Merah. Help from a 'tourist'. Myrmecodia.

The Twin was going to come, but because of the heavy rainfall of the previous night the airstrip was too wet to be able to land on. The Twin had however left from Sentani with a portion of our stuff, but had to instead carry on its flight to Tanah Merah. In the morning we heard the plane fly over, but we could not see it because of the clouds. This didn't help us at all. Alfred van Sprang was also in the Twin (radio reporter and correspondent for the Protestant-Christian weekly, *De Spiegel*) who wanted to come to our camp in the Sibil. Because he was now in Tanah Merah it would probably take a while before he could reach Sibil. Part of our equipment was now also in Tenah Merah but it seemed unlikely that this would be quickly transported to Sibil because the helicopters were not yet flying. We were given some hope when we were told over the radio that a flight had been planned for the Twin to fly to Sibil from Tanah Merah the next day.

Reynders, Vervoort, Verstappen and Herberts went to explore the area around Ok Tsjop and Kiwirok together with the Moejoe carriers.[2] For the carriers there was an extra advantage to joining as they had relatives living in the area, meaning that they would not only earn money, but that they would also be able to visit family. The group was planning on being away for the best part of a week.

That afternoon I collected mosses from around the camp together with my two little friends. At one point, while I was busy collecting I heard one of my friends talking to someone. When I looked up I saw a painted man heavily armed with bow and arrow. He had a big smile on his face and put his hand out for the knuckle greeting. He was very curious as to what I was doing, and so I explained this to him using my hands and feet. Directly after this he too brought me all kinds of mosses. Naturally,

---

[2] The Moejoe carriers were Papuans van the Moejoe tribe in the lowlands which was situated to the South of our basecamp.

I was unable to use all of the material he collected, but in order not to disappoint him I pretended that I was happy with everything he gave me. After a short while he gave me another knuckle greeting and left in the direction of our camp. Because I had never seen this man before, and he was heavily armed it was likely that he had come from afar to visit the camp as a tourist. This happened more often and a member of the closer Kampongs took on the role of tour guide.

Behind our camp in the bushes there were several trees on which some big semi-parasites were growing. These existed of a strong, thick, thorny stem with at the end several green leaves and small flowers. I was curious what these thick stems consisted of and asked my friends to take one down from the tree. I knew something was going to happen as I could see them chuckling together. When I cut the stem in half I saw that inside was a labyrinth of hundreds of small ants. My arms and hands were immediately completely covered, which of course cause some hilarity. Luckily the ants didn't bite and I was easily able to shake them off with the help of my two friends. Later I heard from Kalkman that this ant plant is called a *Myrmecodia*.

Thursday the 23rd of April
Leg wound starts festering. Twin sinks through the grass mat.

After I cut my leg on the trek along the Sibil on the 19th of April I did not really notice the cuts and so, did not pay much attention to them. However, after a couple of days the cuts started to fester and this continued to get worse. To start off with I was still able to walk normally, but this gradually got more difficult. Doctor Romeijn told me to walk as little as possible and cleaned the wounds for me. His assistant, a Papuan he had brought with him from Hollandia gave me a penicillin injection. This assistant was always (overly) well-dressed and based on his attitude you could tell that he felt contempt towards his fellow countrymen. The penicillin injection had to be repeated every day for a week but so far only two injections had been delivered. This meant that the wound was not healing and because of this I had to take the first plane back to Hollandia. In the meantime, I had to keep my leg in a horizontal or upwards position. It seemed silly to me to spend all day sat still when overall I felt just fine. During the days that I was supposed to be resting I did still secretly collect some mosses from the surrounding area of the camp.

The airstrip had dried enough so that the Twin was able to land again to bring the cargo from Tenah Merah. Sadly, everything seemed to be for the cadastre group of which nobody had yet arrived in Sibil. There were also several hundred iron axes which could easily ruin the local market. The bag of post that we had been promised had also not yet arrived. This was very disappointing. We were assured that they would go and pick up another load of cargo. The Twin left again, and after some time returned with a second load of cargo.

To start off with the landing went fluently, but just before the plane got to the end of the airstrip and had slowed down a great deal the left wheel sunk into the grass mat making the plane take a sudden sharp turn to the left and then come to a stop. The lawn which made up the airstrip had not, after all, dried out enough after the heavy rain of two days ago. Luckily there didn't seem to be anything wrong with the plane, but because the wheel had sunk down a lot of earth had collected itself in front of the wheel. This was quickly dug away by several Papuans who laid planks in front of the wheel. An enthusiastic crowd then tried to navigate the plane out of the hole. This would not work, neither would pulling on a long rope which was connected to the plane. The next attempt was to push the tail of the plane towards the airstrip so that this was straight again and adding extra planks under the wheel. After this the motor was turned on so that the plane could pull itself out of the mud. This whole experience cost quite a lot of time and meant that the pilots no longer had enough time to do another trip. This was rather a shame as some of the equipment necessary for our research had still not arrived, like my dry-oven and film rolls. The lawn was immediately repaired by digging out the area around the break and filling the hole with larger rocks from the Sibil river. This was then covered by smaller stones and finished off with clay which was firmly pushed down. The cargo that the Twin had brought with it on the second go did contain the bag of post and part of our equipment. Staats and Van Heijningen received their dissection equipment and were able to start. I received my tripod, which was of very little use until my film rolls came in. Brongersma was relieved that we were finally able to start working. As I didn't want to disappoint him I did not tell him that because I had still not received my dry-oven it was useless for me to start collecting material.

As a special treat all people who were present were given a bar of chocolate. The bars had likely been too warm as they were speckled with white from the cocoa butter. This didn't influence the taste however, and they tasted just fine.

Alfred van Sprang also wanted to travel in the Twin from Tenah Merah to Sibil. Brongersma didn't think this was a good idea at all and persuaded him (through radio contact) to take a Mappiboat (belonging to the oil company) to Kawakit and from there try and get a helicopter to Sibil. Brongersma thought it a lot more important that we received our equipment than that we received a reporter.

Because the Twin was travelling back to Tenah Merah and not to Sentani I still couldn't be brought to a hospital in Hollandia for my leg wound and nobody knew when the next plane would be going to Sentani. I didn't mind this much because my leg wasn't hurting me, though the sitting around was beginning to bore me.

Friday evening the 24th of April
Party in Kigonmedib.

During the day nothing really special happened but in the evening there was a big party in Kigonmedib. Though the kampongwas several kilometres away on the other side of the river we could hear the singing from the party all night long. The noise travelled to us in waves, then relented only to come back even louder later on. A lovely, mysterious singing by these Stone Age people and great to fall asleep to.

Saturday the 25th of April
Herberts group back from Ok Tsjop. A precipice.

Herberts, Reynders, Verstappen and Vervoort had arrived back to our camp after their exploration of the Ok Tsjop area. They had had a good trip and had reached the divide between the Ok Sibil and the Ok Tsjop in the Orion Mountains at a height of about 1900 metres. This area seemed very fitting for botanical and zoological investigation, but because the group did not have enough collection material only a small number of samples had been taken. Twenty-two metres away from the 1800 metre mark Wim Vervoort had however seen some large moss kinds for my collection and brought these with him. More towards the north you were able to see the precipice of the Ok Tsjop. This point had been visited by Jan Sneep previously. He was most likely the first white person to have seen this impressive view. At this point we did not realise that soon enough we would have to climb this precipice from the bottom up.

Anceaux, Pouwer, and De Wilde had arrived back from Kigonmedib where the evening before they had taken part in the party. For them it had been a very interesting experience. They had already learnt some of the language and had been told that this kind of parties were held more often. Later on we would also have ample opportunity to take part in these kinds of festivities.

Sunday the 26th until Tuesday the 28th of April
Film rolls. Forced rest in Sibil. Pavers. Tourism in the camp. The magic of binoculars. Eating in the Silver House. The Sibillers. Cowrie shells as payment. My 'jewellery'. The collection and provisionally drying of mosses. Vervoort's string. Moss collection on fire. The missionaries.

My film rolls and other camera equipment was still lost, so I was unable to take pictures. Via the radio we were alerted that a small package addressed to me had turned up in a small governmental post in the jungle. When asked what needed to be done with it the agreement was made that it would be sent back as soon as another plane came. I supposed that this package may well be my film rolls. It reminded me how Prof. Lam had told me that in the tropics things never go as they should.

The helicopters that were in Tanah Merah were still unable to fly to Sibil because of the clouds in the Songgam Ravine which they needed to fly through and the mountain back over which they had to fly. One of the helicopters couldn't fly either way because the oil pipeline was leaking. In the past week it had rained a lot again and the calm waters of the Sibil had once again turned into a monstrous mud mass.

There was still no end to the forced, eating, drinking, sleeping, do-nothing routine. I had expected the expedition to be very different, however I was placing all my hopes on the third of May as on this day another plane had been planned.

Sometimes I wondered whether it would not have been better if I had arrived in Sibil several weeks later. From a purely scientific point of view this would have been better, however I was happy that we were still so early as it meant that we had ample time and opportunity to properly take in all the new impressions.

During these days I did not investigate any more as this was better for my leg. There was also nothing more interesting to be found in the direct area of the camp and I would not be able to dry it anyway. Instead I found somewhere to sit, with my leg in a horizontal position where I could watch the activities of the Papuans in the camp.

Everywhere I saw men and boys who were busy taking stones from the Sibil River and taking them to the camp in order to create pavement around the camp. Among other things a road was being laid towards the missionary's log cabin. The larger stones were used to make the sides of the path clear and in between this smaller stones were laid as paving.

Jan Sneep told me that for the work they did the men received two packets of matches a day and the boys received one packet. The men also received an axe if they worked for seven consecutive days, for the boys this was 20 days. The matches were trade on throughout the whole of the Sibil Valley and an axe was almost enough to buy a woman with.

From where I had situated myself I discovered all kinds of interesting things. At this point I knew exactly which boys worked hardest and always carried the heaviest stones. Some grown men also carried the big stones. Other men did not actually walk to the river but instead walked to the gate and waited there for a while before taking stones from the boys, which made it seem as if they were working very hard. There were others who only carries small stones. I was pleased to see that the two friends I had made were part of the harder working group. They also came over to me every now and then to ask how I was doing (at least that's what I presume they meant with all their talking).

I was now able to recognise most of the Papuans who were often in the base camp. Every now and then, however, people showed up whom I had never seen before, mostly men and boys. These people were always meticulously dressed up will all kinds of jewellery, like dogs' teeth and cassowary feathers, mostly with their face painted read. They were always armed with a bow and arrow which the Sibillers that we had come to know did not carry. These were clearly tourists, like I had seen in the fields before. They came from kampongs situated further away and had heard that there were many interesting things to be seen in our camp. They wanted to see this for themselves as well. These people were shown around by someone who was often in the camp. Whether or not the guides also received payment I am not sure. One of the guides was Bomdogi, the village elder from the kampong Betabib. He often made jokes and had already learnt how to properly use binoculars. Once he also showed a tourist how to look through binoculars. First he explained exactly how the binoculars should be held and how to look through them, after some practice the tourist would be able to look through the binoculars and see everything properly. At this point Bomdogi already started giggling as he knew that the tourist would jump when everything that was far away suddenly appeared close by. For the tourist this was pure magic and he threw the binoculars on the floor and made a run for it. We never saw anyone run away so quickly. All Bomdogi could do was laugh, and though this was all very entertaining to see I did not find it pleasant to see someone be scared like that.

When dinner was ready a gong sounded and everyone went to the Silver House. The meals were always a distraction and the place where all the news was exchanged. It was always very enjoyable. There were usually several Papuans (not in the dining hall) who hoped that if there was any food left, as was usually the case, they would get this. There was always much talk amongst them, however I never really noticed any real competition in order to get something, though I presume it must have been there. The special smell of the Papuans added aroma to the meals.

The Sibillers

The Sibillers were very friendly, good natured and curious but also extremely helpful, especially the men and boys. During the day people from around the area were almost always present, especially a lot of boys, but also girls, women, and men. The smaller boys usually walked around completely naked, the older boys wore a small tube shaped penis sheath. The girls wore small reed skirts. The men always wore a penis sheath, which was sometimes bent and was attached around their hip with rattan string. They often also wore a black, plaited stomach band and a band around their knee and upper arms. Usually they were carrying a string bag either attached around their head or as a shoulder bag. In order to look extra good, they wore a button on their nose and necklaces made of either dog or pigs teeth and sometimes with cowrie shells, to which they often attached part of a pigs tail. Most men had two small holes on top of the nose through which a stick could be pushed, the end of this stick was then used to attach either the heads of rhinoceros beetles or buttons. The nostrils and septum were also often pierced so that items could be stuck through like pigs tusks, ballpoints, and iodine tubes. To make themselves look especially good they sometimes painted themselves red, while others put red clay in their beard or hair. Their earlobes were often also full of things such as bits of bamboo. It struck me that many of the men had torn earlobes, meaning they had probably attempted to put objects which were too large in their earlobes. Some of the younger men also wore a kind of hat made of cassowary feathers on their head. Sometimes the men were armed with a bow and arrow. The women wore quite a short reed skirt, often several on top of each other. They accessorised with armbands and a band under the knee. They would also sometimes wear necklaces made of cowrie shells. You never saw the women without their carrying nets. I also noticed that especially at the beginning of our stay the women and girls tended to keep close to each other in groups.

The cowrie shells were seen as a legal payment method. Because these are sea shells it shows that there is trade between the people around our camp and the people living on the coast. All of the cowrie shells were in a rather poor state. If the shells had been cleaned and polished there was no longer any interest for them and they were seen as a kind of fake money.

Based on Van der Sleen's suggestion I had brought a great deal of metal wire closers for plastic bags, these were shiny and in bright colours, and could easily be attached to ears, noses, and hair by bending them. I thought that the Papuans may be interested in these as decoration, but the opposite seemed to be true. They didn't even pay attention when I showed them how to wear them. They found other things more interesting like the buttons on the nose and the iodine tubes and ballpoints which they could stick through their nose.

There was also a man who sometimes visited our camp whose top of the nose was loose. When he walked the top of his nose would bounce up and down. It seemed that he had attempted to put something too big through his nose.

It must be made clear here that when you see these things for the first time it makes a lasting impression. Naturally I had seen pictures of Papuans before but that is very different from actually seeing and experiencing in real life. This lasting impression is furthered by the smell of the Papuans. This smell originates from the fat which they often smeared on their bodies. Once I had gotten used to this I did not mind the smell so much and it gave me a homey feeling because I associated it with very friendly and helpful people.

The Papuans were very eager to have their photo taken, especially the boys and men. The women were, initially, often more reticent but once they got to know us properly they became more open and also wanted their picture taken. I do, however, assume that the Papuans did not fully comprehend what photography was. Later on when they were shown the pictures and they recognised themselves this was met with great cheering.

The collection and provisionally drying of the mosses

My task for this expedition was to collect the lower plants such as mosses, lichens and fungi. This task is a lot less easy than it may at first appear. To start off with many species are very small and grow in difficult to reach places, for example, high in trees or on steep cliffs. In some cases serious acrobatics were needed in order to reach a plant. Above all that it is also desirable to collect mosses with spore capsules and finding these can need a rather intense search. Plants which have capsules are often easier to put a name to than those without.

During my collecting I almost always had the help of my two friends. While in the field every sample was put in a separate plastic sandwich bag and labelled with a collection number. The collection information such as location, substrate, height above sea level, sometimes colour etc. which went with every sample were written in a field book.

When the mosses have been collected they need to be dried, if this does not happen they will often start to rot. Most of the collected material consisted of *mussi* and *liverworts*, I only managed to collect a few lichens and fungi and I did not see any algae.

At this point I had been at the basecamp for about two weeks and had hardly managed to collect anything because the dry-oven and my collection material had not yet arrived. I was not at all happy with this and so decided to look into improvising a way to dry as many samples as possible.

To start off with I tried laying the samples on old newspapers on a piece of plastic in the sun. This method did not work as the sun did not shine enough and it was very humid, and the samples were also easily blown away so I had to keep running after them. Sometimes the label blew away as well and I no longer knew which number went with which sample. When this drying method would not work I wrapped the samples with the labels in newspaper and wrote the number on the newspaper as well.

The bigger samples were first split into several packages so that they would be able to dry somewhat more easily. We did not have very many newspapers, and Kalkman needed them to press the higher plants which meant we had to be very economical with our newspaper usage. Because of this I often had to collect smaller samples than I would have wanted to. After I had rewrapped the samples they did not blow away as easily, and if they did it was not a problem as they were all neatly labelled. This method was still not terribly successful because of the lack of sun and the high humidity, but I did not give up and carried on looking for a better method.

In the research barrack an oil drum had been placed in which a fire could be made. The oil drum also radiated heat from the sides so I made a kind of stand close around the drum from wood and other things and placed the moss packages on this stand. When the fire was burning and it was nice and warm the Sibillers always came to warm themselves leaving hardly any space for my mosses and then they frequently fell on the floor due to the crowd. The Sibillers who came to warm themselves worked as carriers, carrying the rocks from the river for paving or strengthening the airstrip. When it was raining they didn't much feel like this and instead came into the research barrack to warm up. We could not really blame them.

Though this method of drying was an improvement, it was still not ideal. I had found a metal lid somewhere and tried to attach this above the fire. To do this I needed something to hang it up with. I had seen that next to where I slept a rope had been strung which would be perfect for the job. This worked quite well, but in order for the mosses to dry properly the lid needed to be quite close to the fire. When new wood was thrown on the fire the flames shot up and burnt through all of my samples and the rope they had been strung up with. This was hilarious to the Sibillers and the flames could clearly be seen from the Silver House meaning I received quite a few comments on the matter. It was not such a big disaster, however, as I still had ample time to re-collect the moss samples. On top of that several of the surviving samples had managed to dry enough to be sent back to Holland. It was clear to me that drying samples without a dry-oven was close to impossible. However, as I did not have one I continued to use the 'metal lid method', though now I did ensure that the lid was further away from the fire.

Later I realised that the rope I had found had been hung up by Wim Vervoort, who slept next to me, probably to dry his washing up on. I had never asked him whether I could use it, though do think that he was rather surly about the matter, though this could also have been my imagination. In hindsight, I should never have used the rope and thought of something else to hang the lid up with.

Although I was forced to sit still I had up to this point still enjoyed myself immensely. In this period, and also later it often crossed my mind how lucky I was that I was able to see what I was seeing first hand.

The Missionaries

I heard from Jan Sneep that the log cabin which I had come across on my first expedition of the area was inhabited by two missionaries. Towards the start of our stay in Sibil I visited once them to introduce myself. They spoke English, but were not very communicative and rather standoffish. I learnt from them that they were here to learn the Papuan language in order to more easily convert the Papuans to Christianity. They grew their own vegetables in an enclosed garden just in front of their house. I was given the impression that they did not feel the need, nor want to have any contact with our group, making it a visit I would not be repeating. During the rest of my time in Sibil we did not hear anything from them, other than a Cessna airplane landing every now and then in order to deliver supplies.

Wednesday the 29th op April
The helicopter is coming.

Via the radio we were informed that the helicopter would try to come from Katem to Sibil. Around twelve o' clock we heard over the radio that the helicopter had actually left Katem. Most of the camp residents went to the airstrip so as not to miss it. Though my leg was still sore I also went. Several people were already sat on the big tree trunk, which had been used for the smoothing out of the airstrip, and staring towards the Songgam valley (Digoel valley) as this was the direction the helicopter should be coming from. It did not look very hopeful as the clouds had collected themselves above the valley and the Orion Mountains. Due to this a lot of people had given up hope that the helicopter would still arrive and had left again. However, around half past twelve we heard the sound of a helicopter nearing and the cheering of the Sibillers. The helicopter had still come, but not from the direction of the valley but from the North-East over the Orion Mountains. Zijlstra, the pilot stepped out of the helicopter, as did Venema the technical leader of the expedition, there was no other useful load. Venema was not met with cheers as the necessary equipment would have been more useful. To decrease the weight of the helicopter the two side doors of the helicopter had been taken off. Zijlstra told us how he had made a navigational error but that he had discovered this in time in order to still turn around and land in the correct place.

Until this point the Papuans had not wanted to believe that things existed which could simply hang in the air, the sight of the helicopter seemed to change their mind. There were a lot of pictures taken of this event, though I did not take any as I only had a sparing amount of film rolls left. After a communal dinner, Zijlstra still felt up to the journey back despite the increasing thickness of the clouds. We were able to give him post with the stamp 'first helicopter flight Sibil-Tanah Merah, 29th of April 1959'. André de Wilde was to leave with the helicopter in order to look for the chest of instruments he desperately needed in Tanah Merah. Because the helicopter was only supposed to fly back the next day a lot of people had not yet prepared their post to give to Zijlstra. However, Zijlstra wanted to leave immediately due to the increasing cloud front. This also meant that I was unable to send my post off as I had not yet prepared it either.

Thursday the 30th of April until the 1st of May
Continued forced rest in Sibil. Mina stole vegetables from the missionaries. A blind boy.

After the exciting events of Wednesday life continued in the camp as normal. From the Silver House I heard Brongersma's typewriter rattling every now and then. In between this I often saw him playing patience, sometimes together with Venema or Van Heijningen. Other than this nothing special happened, other than that the 30th of April was Queensday in Holland. My two friends did come to see me every day to see how my leg was doing.

In the corner of my mosquito net there was a spider web with a nice spider. The spider was a little bit smaller than a garden spider (*Araneus diadematus*) and had two projections on the back of its body, it had been living there since I had arrived in Sibil. This kind of spider was very common in our camp and there were quite a few in our barrack.

Mina, a small Papuan girl came to the Silver House every day while we were eating and was always given the left overs. Until suddenly she stopped coming. Apparently she had stolen food from the missionaries garden. The missionaries had complained to us about it and scared her so much that she was afraid to come to the Silver House.

In the camp I had seen a blind boy several times. He arrived again at the camp again together with his two friends. It was quite touching how he was helped by the other two. They constantly took him by the hand, especially if there was anything he could trip over. Flap, Jan Sneep's dog, was also in the area and the blind boys friend grabbed his hand and stroked the dog with it. Flap thought this was just fine and you could tell by the face of the blind boy that he loved it. This continued until Flap had had enough and wandered off.

Saturday the 2nd of May
Base camp.

There was still no end to our forced rest. Finally, late in the afternoon a Twin arrived from Hollandia with equipment giving us hope that some of the missing items preventing us from collection would arrive. Our hopes were not granted, all of the things which had been brought were unimportant. The relevant and important items such as a box full of medicine for Dr. Romeijn was also not brought even though it had been requested several times through radio contact. My dry-oven, other collection equipment, and photo material did not show up either.

The last week it had rained a lot and the water of the Sibel had changed into a brown mass with a lot of dead wood and tree trunks. It was no longer suitable to swim in. The last two days it had stayed dry, meaning the airstrip could be used again. The helicopters were still not flying to the Sibil on a regular basis. One of the helicopters was still broken and waiting for a necessary part to come from Holland, meaning it would take a while before it would be able to fly again.

Sunday the 3rd of May
Base camp. Twin arriving again.

The Twin was able to make five flights from Sentani today and transport about 4500 kilos of equipment. There is however still a lot waiting for transport to the Sibil. During the unloading the expedition members were stood by full of expectation to see whether or not their own equipment had arrived or whether there was post. There was post, including letters from my mother, Hilly, Uncle Bé and friends. Luckily part of my photography equipment also arrived. Brongersma saw this too and told me that he was happy that I would finally be able to photograph something. This seemed to be slightly questionable as all of my photography equipment had arrived, except my film rolls, meaning I was still unable to take pictures. My dry-oven was also not included, which was to be expected as it had to come from Tanah Merah. Because the last flight only arrived around six in the evening the crew did not want to fly back to Sentani so the Twin stayed in Sibil overnight and planned on flying back the next day. This was the chance for me to go to the hospital in Hollandia to get my tropical sore treated.

We now had the opportunity to write our letters which would also be taken back in the Twin the next day. This meant that everyone was busy writing. I had already started answering my post the day before which meant that I had ample time to finish it off and write about the situation in Sibil. I had also written letters with the stamp of my expedition to my brothers Jan and Gerrit and my uncle Bé.

As most of my ball point pens no longer worked I had to write some of the letters in pencil. I also had issues sealing the aerogrammes, luckily there were several Araucaria trees (*Araucaria*) and I was able to use the wax from these as a kind of glue.

Thinking back about what we had been able to do so far there was little to be said from a scientific viewpoint. Since our arrival in New Guinea, on the 4th of April, a month had gone by in which we had only collected a very small amount. The week in Hollandia did not result in much as the area was very much low land influenced by man where little mosses or lichens grew. In Sibil again, I was only able to do very little because my dry-oven and collection material had still not arrived. I also had to take it easy because of the sores on my leg. During the days that I would be in Hollandia for treatment, I would also not be able to do a lot.

Regardless of these issues I was still very much enjoying my surroundings and was having a very good time. Getting to know the rainforest and the friendly Papuans was a very special and pleasing experience. In the letter that I wrote home on the 2nd of May I literally wrote: "Everything is going as it should and our holiday of doing nothing, eating, and sleeping will not be ending any time soon."

Monday the 4th of May
Taking the Twin to Sentani. Going to the policlinic in Hollandia-Binnen.

In the meantime, the tropical sore on my leg had still not healed due to a lack of medication and I had to get to the hospital in Hollandia as soon as possible. After waiting for about fourteen days I was finally able to go. I gathered some of my essentials and Brongersma gave me some money for any eventualities. I was able to stay in the Governmental Hotel in Hollandia-Binnen again and put the bill on the expeditions tab. Because the plane had only been carrying baggage the chairs had been taken out to make it lighter and to create more space. The pilots fastened me to the floor of the plane, but did so ensuring that I could still look out of the windows and the cockpit. Before we took off I could hear and see the co-pilot go through the necessary proceedings in the script to ensure nothing was being forgotten. They had already put the propellers at the correct angle by hand before starting the plane.

After lift-off we were quickly flying above and between the clouds, sadly I was not able to look down out of the windows from where I was strapped down. As on our flight to Sibil cumulonimbus clouds towered high above the cloud cover. We mostly flew around them, but when they were not too big we went straight through. When we were close to the airport in Sentani the pilots reported to the control tower that they could start warming the coffee. Via the radio it was also passed on that they needed to get an ambulance at the ready. After we landed I was freed from the straps straight away and the ambulance was already waiting for me with wailing sirens. I told the ambulance staff that there was really no need for such a rush, to which they seemed rather relieved. Apparently, they had also just received a call about a woman, who lived in a remote area who was in labour and needed to be taken to the hospital. Now that they no longer needed to rush me to the hospital, they could take us both in one go. We first picked up the woman after which I was dropped off at the policlinic in Hollandia-Binnen, which consisted of several half open barracks. They had already been informed that I would be coming. The doctor who treated me started by cleaning my wound, which involved me keeping my leg is soda water for about half an hour. After this I received a penicillin injection and the wound was bandaged up. I was told that this process had to be repeated every morning. The doctor had a Papuan assistant who had paid great attention to what needed doing so that the next time it needed doing he could do it himself. I was also told that I was not allowed to walk, and had to keep my leg in a horizontal position as much as possible. There was no transport to the hotel, so I had to walk anyway. Luckily the distance was not too great, I estimate it at about 500 metres, so it was quite easy. In the hotel nothing had changed and the lizards were still to be seen everywhere.

Tuesday the 5th of May until Thursday the 14th of May
Hollandia-Binnen. Meerzicht.

Because of the sore I was not able to do much other than stay in the hotel and keep my leg as horizontal as possible. Even though the doctor said I was not allowed to walk, the lack of transport meant I had to walk to the policlinic every day so that the assistant could clean my wound with soda and give me another penicillin injection. The doctor, who sometimes came to take a look, seemed pleased with my progress. Day by day it could be seen that the wound was slowly healing. After a week it had healed so much that I was allowed to walk again. The doctor's treatment room was not much more than a bamboo hut and corrugated iron roof and doubled as a waiting room. During my visits to the policlinic there was also someone with a tropical sore on his hand, which had completely swollen up. The doctor told us that this infection could also be treated but that the healing process would take a lot longer than it did for my leg wound. The doctor also assured us that we should not be worried about the infection.

While I was in the hotel Terco Simon Thomas came to visit me and invited me to join him to Meerzicht, as he had to be in that area for his work. Meerzicht was a recreational area on the Sentani Lake, at the foot of a wooded hill along the road to Sentani. In an area of the lake that had been marked off with buoys you could swim. During the whole day I was the only visitor. I took my time to take a look around, but I wasn't allowed to walk too much so I could not gather any samples. This was not too bad as there probably were not any mosses anyway. This excursion was naturally a welcome change of pace to the rather dull stay in the hotel.

Friday the 15th of May
To Hollandia-Haven.

My leg wound had now healed so much that I could, and was allowed to, walk again. Terco invited me to take a trip with him to Hollandia-Haven, where he showed me all kind of things. We saw another Martin Mariner (the same type of plane we used to fly from Biak to Sentani) land in the water of the Humboldt Bay. The vehicle quickly taxied to the docking area, leaving behind it a trail of splashing water. Along the coast there were several rocks and a row of trees. From these trees I was able to collect several mosses. I not only found several liverworts but also *Calymperes tenerum*, a moss that can be found everywhere along the coast in the tropics.

Saturday the 16th of May
Hollandia-Binnen.

In the morning I only took a look at the area around the hotel, and to actually have something to do I climbed the hill behind the hotel, which I had explored on my last visit. I wasn't able to find anything special but I was able to take some pictures of the area. From here I could see the Sentani Lake as well as the Humboldt Bay.

In the evening I went with Terco to a Chinese restaurant in Hollandia-Binnen. The restaurant was very cosy in the half light from the table lamps. The people who worked in the restaurant were all Chinese and were also very friendly and informal.

Sunday the 17th of May
Hollandia-Binnen.

Now that my leg had completely healed the problem of getting back to Sibil arose. Waiting until the plane would go from Sentani was not much use as it would be several weeks before this happened according to the people on Sentani. I was advised to fly to Tanah Merah first and from there try and get a helicopter belonging to the expedition to fly me to Sibil. Tanah Merah was about 150 kilometres south of our base camp in the low lands and had an airport where flights in a Dakota frequently arrived from Sentani. It would then be a waiting game until a plane would go from Tanah Merah to Sibil. We had heard over the radio that helicopters would not be flying to Sibil for a while due to the cloud front, issues with the mechanics, and sick pilots. After about fourteen days of doing nothing I was ready to leave Hollandia and see what Tanah Merah had to offer me. At this point I called the Sentani airport to ask when the next flight would be, it appeared that this would be on the 19th of May and I immediately reserved a place.

Monday the 18th of May
Pentecostal market of Joka.

In the morning I joined Terco to the kampong Joka situated on the North-East shore of the Sentani Lake at about three kilometres away from Hollandia-Binnen. Here, the traditional Pentecostal market was being held. The houses in Joka were like those in Dojo where we were on our first stay in Hollandia, built above the water. These were situated a lot further away from the shore and could be reached with longer gangways. People from all over brought their merchandise with them in their pirogues. The pirogues were nothing more than hollowed out tree trunks, some of them had a outrigger. The market place itself was a grass field with coconut trees close to the shore of the lake. The merchandise mostly consisted of home grown products, such as bananas and other edibles. Mats and prettily decorated paddles were also being sold. Everything was auctioned off with the language of barter being Malaysian. Everyone was impeccably dressed, a sign that this was an important social event. There was also someone who was selling spears, bows and arrows. These had been painted in bright colours not such a long time ago as the paint had not yet completely dried. Everything happened at quite a slow and steady pace, except for the man selling the spears, bows and arrows as he was loudly trying to sell his merchandise to passers-by. When he saw us he switched to speaking broken Dutch. It is likely that Dutch tourists frequently came to buy souvenirs from the market as it could be reached easily by car. At that moment in time we were the only white people. It was also interesting to see that there were several women smoking thick, home-made cigars. I also saw several women with red mouths from the Sirius plums. Strangely I did not see any men who were smoking. It was also funny to see a black pig running around.

Tuesday the 19th of May
Flight from Sentani via Merauke to Tanah Merah.

I had already been informed the night before how I could get to the Sentani airport most easily. It had been arranged that someone with a Volkswagen who had to be in the area of the airport anyway, would pick me up from the hotel. The car came to pick me up right on time. I had already packed my stuff. Sadly, I had not brought my bag to put everything in with me from Sibil. This is when the rain coat I did have with me came in handy, but not against the rain. I used it to put all of my stuff in and tied it up as a sort of bundle. It was a strange piece of baggage but luckily they did not say anything about it at the airport during the weigh in.

After take-off we were quickly flying above the clouds again. The cloud front did show holes here and there, but not much could be seen as the Dakota was flying at about 5000 metres. After some time, the visibility improved and the central mountain range loomed before us which was now bathed in sunlight. After a short time, we flew right over the Sibil

Valley, but were too high to be able to see the camp. I could however clearly see the mass of Antares. It was a nice idea that I was now in the plane that we had heard fly over Sibil so often but had never managed to see. From this height it became very much clear how spread out but also how traitorous the Central Range actually was. Everywhere I could see steep, wooded slopes and deep ravines. In some places it could be clearly seen that the steep slopes had no trees on them at all, which I presume was caused by the landslides. Soon after this the landscape changed into endless low land rainforest, in which several, wide meandering rivers could be seen like silver ribbon. At this point I did not know that soon enough I would be spending weeks trekking through this rainforest and the rough mountain area to reach the Sibil Valley. I presumed that we would now quickly start descent into Tanah Merah but we kept flying at the same height. I even wondered whether I was actually in the right plane, but on my ticket it clearly said Tanah Merah and this had been checked before I had boarded. After almost another hour of flying I saw the sea looming, after which I saw houses and the airport of Merauke. After we landed we all had to get out of the plane, also the passengers for Tanah Merah. All of the baggage, including my bundled raincoat was also unloaded and placed on the floor close to the plane. The passengers for Merauke were allowed to take their luggage and everything that was left was reloaded into the plane. The passengers for Tanah Merah were also allowed to board the plane again. Next to the airstrip I saw several small, burnt out planes. I presume that they were left over from the Second World War and were most likely American fighter jets. They could not be Japanese planes, as Merauke was never occupied by the Japanese. We flew back, and after less than an hour we started our descent and landed on the airport (lawn) of Tanah Merah. There was a whole welcoming committee stood ready, but of course they were not there solely for me. Later I noticed that whenever a plane came, which was several times a week, a large group of people came to watch. There was a jeep with a trailer waiting to take what little passengers there were and their baggage to the centre of Tanah Merah, a distance which couldn't have been more than several hundred metres. The driver was very proud to tell us that they had only just purchased the car, and that before this the transport had been done on the back of a bicycle or by a cart pulled by the locals. It did not take long for someone to strike up a conversation with me. This was Mr. Fanoy, Head of Local Governance (H.P.B.) who asked me whether I had already discussed shelter. Because I had not yet arranged anything, he arranged a place for me in the local prison while he waited for a more suitable place. At the same moment that our plane had landed a boat had moored with supplies for Tanah Merah. Mr Fanoy had to leave to deal with this directly, but said that he would contact me the following day. Of course I did not know where the prison was, but a couple of Papuans took my luggage and brought me there. Altogether it had been quite a tiring day, and I went to bed early. It was a fun idea that this would be the first time I would actually sleep in a prison.

Wednesday the 20th of May
Tanah Merah. Collecting trip towards Mindiptana. Swapping a pipe.
In the morning I first took a look around the prison, as I was able to walk everywhere freely. It was a square enclosed area with several unmanned look out towers. I did not notice any prisoners though there were people walking around who greeted me in a friendly manner. Whether these were the prisoners or not never became clear. It seemed to be no problem at all, that I, someone who had nothing to do with the prison was walking around in it freely. Tanah Merah itself was made up of several aligned streets, surrounded by Casuarina trees and detached houses. The first moss that I found here (*Hypophila involuta*) was abundantly growing in the cement drainage chute at the marines' barracks. While I was in the chute to collect the moss I was approached by a marine. He already knew who I was and must have thought that there was something wrong with me. I explained to him what I was doing in the chute. He told me that I could stay in the barracks and brought me there. I was shown to a bed in a room with several other marines. For the meals I was also allowed to join the marines, and this is what I did for the following days.

I had heard that they were busy creating a road through the forest from Tanah Merah to Mindiptana, a distance of about 50 kilometres. I presumed that this would by me best chance to enter the real primary rainforest. I quickly found the road and walked down it. It was a broad, unhardened and slippery road and the rainforest started close to Tanah Merah. Along the first part of the path there were several gardens, some of which had been enclosed and others had not. I was not able to see what was being grown in the enclosed gardens, but in the gardens that were not enclosed I mostly saw cassava, keladi (an arum-like plant of which the underground tubers were eaten), sugar cane and bananas. I was being followed by several Papaun boys who kept themselves at a discreet distance whilst talking and laughing with each other. I had experienced the same thing in the Sibil, and what you had to do was give them something to eat and say something to them. I always carried several kaki's with me (type of biscuit) so I gave all of the boys some of these. After this all their hesitation vanished. They spoke a couple of words of Dutch and through this I was able to explain to them what I was doing. Of course they also immediately started looking. Though this was good fun, they usually only collected the larger species meaning I still had to continue looking for the smaller kinds. The boys spent the whole day with me, and carried all of my stuff. On the bare ground of the road a lot of pitcher plants could be found, other than this I did not see many flowering plants in the area.

I did however come across three adult Papuans, two men and a woman who were coming from the direction of Tanah Merah. They too kept their distance until I offered them some kaki's. At that point they moved closer and also seemed very interested in what I was doing. The woman was wearing only a grass skirt, one of the men was wearing short trousers and a vest, and the other was wearing only a 'nutshell' part of a callabas as a penis sheath. The group was clearly not from Tanah Merah as they were armed with bow and arrow. The fact that the man was wearing a nutshell instead of a longer sheath was also a sign that they were making a long journey. It was clear from the kind of skirt the woman was wearing that they were from the lowlands, this because her skirt was knee length and made of flexible grass swaying as she walked. In the mountain area women wore much shorter skirts made of reed which is a lot more stiff. All three of them had a carrying net as I knew them in Sibil. The man with the short trousers was carrying an iron axe which he had probably swapped for home grown fruits or tubers. He also had two wooden containers hanging on string in his hand, in one of the containers he was carrying young keladi plants and in the other young sugar cane plants, naturally meant to be used to continue growth in your own garden.

The road ended after about 12 kilometres. At the endpoint several Papuans were busy chopping down a tree. One of them stopped us from coming closer as a large tree was about to come down. All men ran away on command and slowly the tree started to fall down and landed with a loud creaking noise on other trees and eventually on the floor. This was a good opportunity for the men to rest and tell me all kinds of things that I sadly didn't really understand. They were very friendly and extremely curious as to what I was doing. One of them squatted down and started smoking a pipe. The pipe itself was rather interesting and was made up off a small tube about as big as a cigarette in which tobacco could be placed this smaller tube slotted in to a finely decorated wooden tube of about 30 centimetres which had a closed off end. He made clear to me that I could have the pipe in return for the bag full of kaki's I still had left. Of course, I did this and everyone was happy. The road workers spent the night under small shelters made of sticks and covered with leaves. Smoke was coming from one of these shelters, clearly they were busy preparing dinner. Every time the road had been lengthened by a little bit the shelters were broken down and built up again. Here, the rainforest largely consisted of rather thin trees with a height of about 15 to 20 metres. Scattered here and there were slightly thicker and taller trees. The undergrowth was not very thick, and there weren't that many dead trees either. The moss growth was also rather limited. The most useful parts were the thin twigs close to the ground and several of the rotting tree trunks and buttress roots. On the way back I did not have to carry anything, instead the boys carried all of the plastic bags with the collected material and my bags, full of pride.

Naturally I took pictures of this journey. My camera (the Rolleycord) had a big square shutter which you had to look in from the top to focus. This had the possibility of causing issues as the temperature and humidity was so high that drops of sweat were constantly falling onto the shutter which then had to be cleaned first in order to get a clear picture. In the evening I placed my collected mosses in the sleeping area on newspapers in order to dry. I explained to the marines whom I shared the room with what I was going to do with the mosses and what the goal and point of my research was. I do not believe that all of them understood this properly, though some of them seemed to find it interesting. One of the marines made the remark that they were now at least finally experiencing something, which must be a sign that they were extremely bored. We were able to get along rather well, so afterwards we all sat and talked for a while before going to sleep.

Thursday the 21st of May
Tanah Merah. Found my dry-oven. Big hairy spider in sleeping quarters.

I spent the day exploring Tanah Merah some more. Close by there were several other kampongs. I walked to one of them together with the boys from the day before. The kampong was made up of a broad middle path with bamboo houses on either side situated on poles of about a metre high and roofs covered with leaves from the nipa palm. Next to some of the houses a rusty oil drum had been placed to collect the water from the roof. In front of one of the houses a man was busy plaiting the leaves of the nipa palm into roofing. He was proud to show me how it was done. I saw a lot of children everywhere, but other than the leaf plaiter I did not see any adults. I presume that they were working on their gardens or in Tanah Merah. As qthere was nothing for me to collect here, I returned back to Tanah Merah almost immediately.

Most of the Papuans in Tanah Merah wore shorts, some of them also wore a vest or t-shirt (often with a rip) and only a few had a penis sheath. I think that those who did wear a penis sheath did not live in Tanah Merah but were either visiting or trading. The smaller boys walked around either completely naked or also in shorts. The smaller girls almost all walked around in a small grass skirt. Some of the women wore a dress, though quite a lot still only wore the grass skirts. The skirts here were longer than those in Sibil and almost reached the knees, like the skirt of the woman I had previously met.

I went on to the airport to see whether I could find my dry-oven anywhere. Upon my arrival I saw one of the expedition's helicopters, but no sign of the crew. Certain parts of the helicopter had been wrapped in tarp; not a sign that they would be flying any time soon. There were several small hangars by the airport I was able to simply walk in, in here I found several cases marked 'Sibil'. With the help of someone who worked there we opened the cases rather easily. To my delight my dry-oven and hurricane lamps appeared. I unpacked these to take with me.

I was told here that the jeep with its trailer was the only car in Tanah Merah, something which I had also been told by the driver upon my arrival. I was told that the jeep had been bought by the expedition in order to take the necessary materials which were delivered by boat in Tanah Merah from the dock at the Digoel to the goedang (warehouse) in Tanah Merah, or the hangars by the airport. To me this seemed a very expensive investment as the distance was only several hundred metres. I am sure I could have thought of a cheaper way of doing it.

I had discovered earlier on that there was a painting hung on the wall of our barrack on a somewhat crooked wooden frame. From behind this frame part of a hairy leg was sticking out. Upon closer inspection this leg appeared to belong to a spider who must have been about 6 centimetres wide. When I looked behind the painting the spider just stayed put. The marines said that they had seen the spider before and that it had been sat in the same position for days. I too let him be, I did however make sure that my mosquito net was properly fastened to my bed at night.

Friday the 22nd of May
Tanah Merah.

Tanah Merah is situated by the wide Digoel River and I figured that I could just as well go and have a look at the docking areas, as I had nothing better to do. Along and in the river a group of boys was playing. I asked them if there were also crocodiles in the river. They told me that this was the case, but that they were only small and didn't do anything.

Along the backwater of the Digoel I discovered an area where people dug river gravel. There were also areas, just above the water where people could wash their clothes. In the water there were several hollowed out tree trunks used as pirogues.

Slowly I was becoming rather bored with Tanah Merah. I did however see a hornbill in one of the Casuarina trees in the centre of town. These are the birds who have a big banana shape on their beak. I had seen pictures of them before but this was the first time I had seen one in real life.

Some of the marines bartered with the Papuan women dressed in grass skirts. They sold fruits such as bananas for money. The women did not enter the barracks but instead traded through a hole which had been made in the fence surrounding the compound.

The only news that we heard in Tanah Merah was via the radio. All kinds of outposts were able to send their regards, place orders, have conversations with their family, or ask for medical advice. The whole of New Guinea could listen in on this, and this was often done. Sometimes the men who were about to start a private conversation with his wife would begin with 'Good morning listeners'. I never used to listen to the radio, however the marines always informed me if there was news from Brongersma in the Sibil. Today we were informed that Van der Weiden, head of the land registry team in Sibil would soon be coming to Tanah Merah to charter about 100 Moejoe carriers. He could not do much in the Sibil because a lot of his equipment was still in Tanah Merah and it still didn't look like the helicopters would be ready any time soon. This is why he had decided to travel to Tanah Merah himself and then walk back to Sibil with the Moejoe carriers and the most important equipment for his research.

Saturday the 23rd of May
Tanah Merah. Ordered extra film rolls. Still no helicopters to Sibil. Indonesian parachutists dropped?

There is not much to be said about this day either. I was able to collect several mosses, but these were probably the same kind as on the previous days. After another visit to the marines' canteen I busied myself with drying the collected mosses. This was now properly possible by laying them on newspapers on the floor of our barrack. This never caused any issues with the marines and they made sure to walk around them. When the mosses had been dried sufficiently I packaged them in newspapers together with their assigned number. The data was registered in a field book.

My stock of film rolls was beginning to run out and I could see it coming that I wouldn't have enough. Because of this I went to the post office to send a telegram to Jos Lange (from the photography store) and ask him whether he could send 10 new film rolls as quickly as possible. As I had agreed this with him previously, he knew exactly what type of film rolls I needed.

After this I went back to the airport because I could hear the sound of a helicopter. My ears did not deceive me, and one of the pilots (Zijlstra) was busy testing the helicopter. He told me that the helicopters would be able to fly to Kawakit and Katem but that it would take a while before they could fly to the Sibil again. My conversation with him gave me the impression that he was not really motivated to find a way to fly to Sibil as soon as possible.

After this I put some effort into finding some more samples in the area.

That afternoon the Dakota from Merauke would also be arriving. The plane arrived, promptly on schedule, but the landing did not go exactly as planned as the plane was still going too fast when it came to the end of the slightly upwards sloping airstrip. The motors were put back to maximum and the Dakota made another lap and proceeded to land perfectly.

I was slowly beginning to feel like a marine, I slept with them, ate with them, and had nothing to do, like them. On top of this my khaki coloured trousers and shirt somewhat resembled their uniform. The biggest difference was that I did not have to turn up to the roll call every morning. In the evening there was a dispute with the sergeant of my group of marines. There were rumours going around that not far from Tanah Merah several Indonesian military had been dropped. The discussion was about whether or not the Dutch Marines should actively try and track them down and attack them, or whether they should do nothing. The decision was made quite quickly that there was no point in trying to track them down. For starters we were not even sure that they were there and if they were there we probably would not be able to find them anyway. Why risk your own life for something that could not be done in any case? Luckily the conclusion was made that nothing should be done about them.

Sunday the 24th of May
Boattrip to Kaliwin and Ajerok. The most desolate place.

The doctor in Tanah Merah, Doctor Bijkerk, often took boat trips to several kampongs downstream of the digoel and upstream along the tributary Mandobbo. He had asked me the day before whether I would like to join him on one of these trips, naturally this was not an opportunity I would let slide. Early in the morning at the agreed time (about eight) the boat was ready to go and the crew, (all Papuans) were busy making the final preparations. Doctor Bijkerk and his assistant joined shortly after I arrived with the medicine bag. The captain and his mate could be recognised by their white socks and army boots they were wearing. Though it was only a small boat the crew still consisted of eight people. I presumed that there must also be several passengers included in this who were interested in taking a ride as well. I liked the idea of this, after all, the more the merrier. The boat was completely open and did not have a cabin, but did have a roof made of tarp.

    The first kampong we arrived at was Kaliwin, which was situated on the Digoel about 10 kilometres downstream from Tanah Merah. The boat was fastened to the pier and because the water was so low we were able to jump straight out of the boat. From the pier you could see that the water could also reach much higher. The kampong was very much like the kampong close to Tanah Merah that I had visited earlier. Here again there was a broad street with bamboo houses and roofing made of leaves from the nipa Palm. Here and thee nipa palms had been planted close to the houses so that the roofing materials were easily accessible. Again there were also several rusty drums to catch the water running off the roofs. There did not seem to be many people around at all, though there were several dogs. This also meant that Doctor Bijkerk did not have much to do and we quickly proceeded downstream again. The Digoel River must have been about 200 metres wide and meandered strongly. From the boat we had a magnificent view of the rainforest which in most areas reached right up to the water. In the inside corners of the river there were sometimes rather broad sand banks. The rainforest must have been about 20 metres high, with here and there trees which must have been double this. We saw white herons along the banks several times and also saw white cockatoos in the air which strongly contrasted against the dark green of the rainforest. I presume that these were the same kind as I had seen from the plane when flying to Sibil. Other than white cockatoos we also saw several much larger, black ones with a red head. We also saw two big, loudly squawking hornbills flying over. In several places along the shore there were several houses built on higher land. Often the home grown nipa palms, banana trees and less frequently tall sago palms could also be seen here. If the inhabitants of these houses were at home, they would come out and excitedly wave and shout. In several areas, close to the shore there were mixtures of low growing plants and several banana trees. No houses could be seen here, but it could be seen that there once had been. At one point we passed a shelter where there were several canoes, we were told that this was the general crossing, and that everyone was allowed to use these canoes as long as they left them where they were. After several hours we saw the tributary of the Digoel to the left, this was the Mandabbo which we took on our way to Ajerok, our main point of destination. This river was still rather wide though clearly less so than the Digoel.

On our way Doctor Bijkerk wanted to stop by a man whom he always visited when he passed on his way to Ajerok. This man lived by himself in a detached pile house. The house was very much dilapidated and wonky on high poles. Smoke came through the roof but other than this there was no sign of life. You could only enter the house through a hole in the floor through which a tree trunk fashioned into a ladder had been stuck. Together with Doctor Bijkerk I climbed into the house while shouting for the man. Other than the still smoking fire nothing could be seen, the owner had most likely left shortly before we arrived. Doctor Bijkerk found this odd as before the man had always returned to his house when he heard a boat coming. To me this place was the most desolate place in New Guinea that I had seen so far. As far as the eye could see there was only a green sea of rainforest through which only the thin strip of the Mandabbo could be distinguished. The house stood completely alone on a plot of cut down trees were the trunks still stuck out like skeletons above the other plant life. There was no colour or flower to be seen anywhere and on top of this the desolation was only enhanced by the cloudy skies. The image gave me the feeling that an atom bomb had just fallen which had destroyed all life. We waited there for several minutes but nobody showed up so in the end we continued our journey to Ajerok.

Now and again rather big tree trunks floated by which the mate graciously managed to avoid. He told us that at the moment there were a lot less tree trunks in the water than when the water was risen, making avoiding them a lot harder. On our way we came past canoes and their rowers several times who waved at us enthusiastically. In many places there were horizontally growing mossy tree trunks just above the water, because our boat could easily be manoeuvred we were able to sail towards these so that I could collect samples.[3] After a short while we

---

3 Later this turned out to be a new species to science (*Sematophyllum mandobboense* Zanten spec. nov.)

moored at Ajerok at what seemed to be a pier in process. They were busy building a platform high above the water, another sign that the water was able to rise lot higher than it had now. The sun had started to shine making everything look a lot happier. Close to the pier there was a rather big and neat bamboo house with a roof of nipa leaves which was used as a passanggrahan (local hotel). Like in Kaliwin we first had to walk up a slope to reach the kampong. The kampong consisted of a big square surrounded by bamboo houses, nipa palms and banana trees. In a lading (garden) close to the kampong cassava was being cultivated. The villagers that were present, mostly women, children and dogs came up to meet us. It seemed that they already knew that Doctor Bijkerk would be coming. It would take him a while to treat the Papuans and while he was doing this I had ample opportunity to explore the kampong and the area around it. Three Papuans who had also come with us on the boat stayed with me. The women and children from the kampong found us very interesting and all wanted their pictures taken. One of the women had a large lump on her stomach, of which Dr. Bijkerk wasn't sure what it was, however it didn't seem to bother her at all. Another woman was suffering from tuberculosis and received an injection, which she received with a smile on her face. Doctor Bijkerk told me how there was a lot of tuberculosis in this area. In order to fight this a screening programme had been started not so long ago in Getenteri situated further downstream on the Digoel. Hundreds of people had come to this to get themselves X-rayed.

Close by the village a piece of forest had been chopped down to create a cemetery. All of the graves had been given a shelter to ensure that the rain would not wash away the soil. The cemetery was almost completely surrounded by cassava crops. After this me and my three guides entered the real rainforest in order to collect some samples. Most kinds could be found on rotting wood, trunks and on buttress roots of which there were several sorts of low land species such as *Calymperes, Syrrhopodon,* and *Leucobryum*. Some of these kinds also appeared to be new to science. On thin twigs in the undergrowth we also found a couple of pleurocarpus mosses. The total count of different species was however rather low. The three Papuans helped me collect the specimens so in no time all of the bags had been filled. After this we went back to the boat where the others were waiting for us.

It was noticeable to me that in this area the kampongs looked so neat. According to Dr. Bijkerk this was only recently the case. Due to the government a lot of improvements had been made with regards to hygiene, house building, and medical supplies. Before this the kampongs were a lot messier and the houses were stood on very high poles, like the one we had seen one on our way to Kaliwin. The high poles aided in defence against enemies. Now that there were no enemies in the area the houses also no longer needed to be built on the high poles.

We got back on the boat and sailed back to Tanah Merah, where we arrived just before dark. I was of course very much satisfied with the day as I had seen and experienced a lot of new things. Above all I was now able to add some moss kinds to my collection which I had not yet come across.

Monday the 25th until Thursday the 28th of May
Tanah Merah.

Nothing special really happened during this period. After the first successful attempt of a helicopter to reach the Sibil on the 29th of April it had not happened again. I had also not received any letters from home in weeks, the letters were probably in Sibil where I had been absent for more than a month, or still in the post office in Hollandia.

Life with the marines was still pleasant. They were all very friendly and helpful, however conversations remained rather distanced. I was enjoying myself just fine as a 'marine' as I was allowed to do as I pleased in what must be said was a very special location. But I had not come here to have a vacation, so the life here slowly began to bore me.

In the meantime, I had gotten through all of my rolls of film, meaning I was unable to take any more pictures. Via the radio I heard that the rolls of film which had been previously misplaced had been found in the middle of nowhere and would be sent to Sibil. At this point that did not help me at all. Because all of the radio messages in New Guinea could be heard by everyone, the whole of New Guinea must have known that my film rolls had been found.

Friday the 29th of May
Tanah Merah. Collecting higher plants.

My stay in Tanah Merah was starting to get monotonous and I was getting extremely bored. I could not find any new mosses anywhere so instead I started collecting higher plants. In Tanah Merah there were more than enough available newspapers needed to dry the specimens. On the 22nd, 23rd, and 24th of May I had already collected some higher plants from the sides of the road in Tanah Merah. Specialists at the Rijksherbarium in Leiden later informed me that these were mostly common weeds. This time I was looking in the area of the air strip. Here I found one plant, a *Cyparecae* that I thought looked interesting enough to collect. The plant grew along a shallow ditch off the side of the lawn of the airstrip.[4]

Saturday the 30th of May
Tanah Merah.

I looked through the whole area of Tanah Merah to see whether there were any mosses which I could add to my collection. I especially looked on the trunks and twigs of trees. There can't have been many trees that I missed. There was a large jack tree on the military grounds covered for a large part in fern, there was also a large mango tree. These supplied me with several liverworts and two kinds of byopsida (*Ectropotheciopsis novo-guineensis* and *Meiothcium microcaroum*) which I had not seen before.

---

4   Later this specimen was examined by Dr. Kern from the Rijksherbarium in Leiden and determined as a *Fimbristylis leptoclada* (new to New Guinea) and was a so far undescribed variety, described by him as *F. leptoclada* var. *etuberculata* Kern. var. nov.

Sunday the 31st of May
Tanah Merah. Van der Weiden (Fred) arrives. A course in rainforest walking. Two routes to the Sibil. Preparation walk to Sibil. Bodyguard.

Van der Weiden (Fred) arrived from Sibil in Tanah Merah. Part of the journey from the basecamp to Katem through the Songgam Valley he had walked because the helicopters were not yet able to fly this route. From Katem to Tanah Merah the helicopters were flying and Fred had made use of these to finally arrive in Tanah Merah. Meeting Fred was very enjoyable and it seemed that from the start we got along well with each other. It did not take us long to address each other on a first name basis and we spent a lot of time with each other talking about all kinds of things, but especially a lot about his experiences in the rainforest. It was from him that I learnt a lot about the rainforest and what you should or should not do in certain situations.

For the land register he had to determine the exact location with a sextant. For this he could make good use of the facilities at the base camp and in Antares. Because the expedition was close to the border of Australian New Guinea it was especially important to determine where the border was between the two.

Fred did not trust the helicopters and much preferred using carriers. He wanted to bring a group of Moejoe carriers with him. He would need them not only for the trek to Sibil, but also for his research into the location by the Antares. His motto was that carriers were always trustworthy and helicopters were not.

He had come to Tanah Merah to charter a group of a 100 Moejoe carriers to come with him to Sibil. He had shown me how he had arrived at this number of carriers for this trip. It is a rule that every carrier eats about 35% of what he is carrying in a week. The journey to the basecamp could be made in about 10 days, but because delays were always a possibility it was better to go by 14 days. This meant that every carrier was only left with about 30% of useful load.

If I ever wanted to return to the Sibil I need not wait any longer for a helicopter; he advised me to join him and his carriers on their journey. This seemed to me like a great idea and I immediately said yes without thinking about it. I had already heard from one of the marines in my barrack that Fred would ask me to join him. The marine had literally said to me "Mister Van der Weiden likes you a lot and he would like it very much if you would join him on his journey to the Sibil."

Fred worked independently and organised the material he needed for his research himself. He had had experience with this kind of thing before so he was trusted to handle it all by himself. It surprised me how he managed to arrange all that needed to be done. With everyone who he needed to do something he first had an informal friendly talk. Sometimes this happened in an office, belonging to the post or governmental officials, but normally there was no one there not even in office hours, but during a walk in Tanah Merah you normally ended up running into someone you were looking for. Casually, and while drinking a beer he would tell you what he needed. His motto was always drink as many beers as you can in the heat, as soon as you're in the field you won't be able to any more. He was never in a rush, and often said "if you can't arrange things today you can arrange them tomorrow." He told me all kinds of details about our upcoming journey to Sibil. Certain necessary aspects of the journey and his stay in Sibil had already been arranged which I was rather pleased about as, I myself had no idea what would have to be arranged and who would be able to help you with that. It would take about two and a half to three weeks to walk the 150-kilometre route to the Sibil' but because of possible delays the estimation was made at three and a half weeks. The most important food we needed to bring was of course rice, but the toko in Tanah Merah did not have enough supplies for our whole group, so Fred had ordered it in advance so that there would be enough. We also needed a big sail to sleep under. The materials of our research could not be forgotten, for me this largely consisted of my dry-oven and hurricane lamps that I had recovered from the airport and paper bags in which collected material could be dried. We also needed enough petroleum for the lamps. Fred said that he did not care how heavy or tiring the journey was as long as he slept well at night, but that he could only do this in his own bed. For this he had had a bed made of aluminium that could be taken apart into two pieces. For all of this baggage and a lot more Fred said we needed about 100 carriers. These had been discussed by him before and came from the watershed of the Kaoh and the Moejoe (tributaries of the Digoel). They arrived in Tanah Merah, if I remember correctly, on the 2nd or 3rd of June.

There were two routes which went from Tanah Merah to the Sibil, the western and the eastern route. The western route was slightly shorter but the first part needed to be done by use of a Mappiboat belonging to an oil company. It would take extra time to try and arrange such a boat, if this would work at all. This route also went through more uninhabited areas which were undesirable with regards to sleeping arrangements. The eastern route, which was also used to carry materials for the expedition by helicopter, went through more populated areas with several kampongs. These kampongs were interconnected by relatively good routes. Because of these reasons Fred chose to take the eastern route, which also went straight through the Moejoe area where our carriers came from. About a month earlier this route had also been walked by Jan Sneep, André de Wilde and Cees Kalkman. Jaap Reynders had passed this area just before us on his way to the Sibil with about 50 Moejoe carriers. Because the journey went mostly through Moejoe area our carriers would be able to act as interpreters.

The first part of the area we would be trekking through had only recently come under governance, meaning that it was possible that some skirmishes could take place. Because of this we first had to ask the governing powers of Tanah Merah for their permission to go on our journey. We could only have permission if two members of the Papuan police force would join us on our costs. These officers were armed with a gun and were under orders not to let me, or Fred out of their sight. I quite liked the idea of getting our own bodyguards, however it seemed somewhat over the top safety wise, as I had not once felt unsafe on any of my travels.

Monday the 1st of June
Saying goodbye to Tanah Merah.

While waiting to leave on our journey to the Sibil I spent some time wandering around Tanah Merah to see whether there was anything interesting to collect. Sadly, I found hardly anything, I could not find a single new moss type and only found one higher plant, a *Calopogon* that seemed interesting enough to take with me.

Tuesday the 2nd of June
Tanah Merah. Day of rest. Readying collected material for shipment.

Fred advised me to do as little as possible in the days before the journey in order to preserve strength. I spent the whole day sorting out the mosses that I had collected in Tanah Merah and the surrounding area and getting them ready to ship to Holland.

Wednesday the 3rd of June
Tanah Merah. Receiving letters and rolls of film from home. Rude letter from Uncle Wout. What was happening in Sibil in the meantime.

The Dakota arrived again today with the post. There were several letters for me from home, of which two were from Hilly and Jan and a rather rude letter from my Uncle Wout. He accused me, in a very aggressive manner that I was neglecting him and my mother by not sending them letters frequently enough. He also stated that he presumed that he would not hear anything from me at all after this letter. Of course, I did reply to his letter and explained to him how the mail service worked here and that it was simply not possible to send letters more often. Sadly, there were no film rolls included in the post. A bit later the delivery man came back with another package that had been in the bag with letters. To my relief these were the film rolls from Jos Lange that I had ordered through telegraph. This meant I would be able to take pictures of the coming journey to the Sibil. I also received a letter from Jos Lange in which he informed me that some of the black and white pictures had a bright mark on them and that this was probably due to the camera not closing properly. He also advised me, after looking at the negatives that I had sent him, that the negatives featuring Papuans could do with longer lighting because of their dark skin colour.

I did not know what exactly was happening in Sibil, the only information we received in Tanah Merah was via the radio which was broadcasted through the whole of Dutch New Guinea. The signal was often poor and creaky, sometimes it completely stopped or other people would be talking through it. What we did gather from the information we received was that the food was almost all gone and that in order to avoid hunger foodstuff had been dropped from a Dakota flying over. This cost the expedition 25.000 guilder which had not been part of the calculations. The Dakota couldn't land in Sibil because the air strip was too short. We also gathered from the radio contact that the group that was chopping down a path to the Antaras, led by geologist Bär had had to return to the camp because the helicopters were unable to provide them with supplies. The big problem was not the lack of food but rather the fact that the helicopters were continuously unable to fly to provide for the groups in the field. At this point both pilots were sick with jaundice and had been taken to the hospital in Hollandia. To replace them an extra mechanic and helicopter pilot were going to come from Holland. The new pilot would have to accustom himself to the route still which would take a while when flying was only possible if it is not too cloudy. This meant that the chance that the helicopters would be able to fly to the base camp any time soon was rather slim. Because of all of these issues Brongersma was considering moving the basecamp to Katem, which was only 200 metres above sea level. For me this was not a very good idea as my research required me to go to the higher mountain ranges.

Thursday the 4ᵗʰ of June
Tanah Merah. Change in plans for the journey to the Sibil.

The plans for walking to the Sibil were slightly changed. Originally the idea was to walk from Tanah Merah to Mindiptana. This would take about three days along trickily navigated paths created by the locals, and through the low land forest. The first part of the journey would then be along the road in process, which I had already walked to the end of at the beginning of my visit to Tanah Merah. However, by chance the resident of South New Guinea (A. Boendermaker) would be visiting Getenteri and Mindiptana by boat from Tanah Merah. We could take the boat with him to Mindiptana. This saved us a couple of days of walking through a rather boring piece of wood. The carriers with the baggage would not all be able to fit on the boat so they still had to walk the distance according to the original plan.

Friday the 5ᵗʰ of June
Tanah Merah. Carriers leave for Mindiptana and Woropko.

We didn't have anything to do, together with Fred I walked around Tanah Merah and we started saying our goodbyes to the marines and our other acquaintances, but this couldn't fill up the whole day. I also wrote letters home informing them about my looming journey. In the marine's canteen there was an old typewriter that I could use. Though this had a rather old and faded tape the result was still better than my hand written letters in pencil. All of my ball points still refused to work.

Early in the morning our carriers left for the two-day journey to Mindiptana. We double checked that Van der Weiden's bed and my dry-oven had really been packed, and it all seemed to be in order. We waved the group off and would meet them again two days later in Mindiptana.

Saturday the 6th of June
Boat journey from Tanah Merah to Getenteri on the Digoel. Mosquitoes and smelly socks.

This was the day that we left for Getenteri and Mindiptana in the government's boat called the *Tasman*. It was a much larger boat than we had previously taken to Ajerok, and there were a lot of people on it. Along with the crew and the resident of South New Guinea, Mr. A. Boendermaker, there were also several marines, I presume to protect the resident. Our two bodyguards (armed Papuan officers) were also on the boat and some other Papuans of whose function I did not know. Part of the journey up until the confluence with the Mandabbo I had sailed before when I went to Kaliwin and Ajerok with Dr. Bijkerk. This time we continued sailing along the Digoel to the point where the Kaoh (also called Oewimmerah) flowed into the Digoel. It was here that the kampong Getenteri was situated. The distance from Tanah Merah to Getenteri was 50 kilometres as the bird flies but because of the many meanders we must have sailed at least double the distance. Towards the end of the afternoon we arrived in Getenteri, a beautifully situated kampong on a hill with a wonderful view of the confluence of the Kaoh and Digoel river. A government and mission post had been situated here and it was a lot more modern than Tanah Merah. The resident and his party spent the night in Getenteri. We were also able to spend the night in Getenteri which Fred did as his bed was travelling with the carriers.

I much preferred to sleep with the Papuans on the boat. I only spent a short amount of time in the kampong as it had started to get dark and I wanted to ready my sleeping area on the boat. The boat was anchored in a curve of the Koah close to the shore. I slept, with a few of the Papuans on the roof of the boat. The only thing I had to do was attach my mosquito net to any of the protrusions I could find. Most of the Papuans sleeping in the boat did not have a mosquito net. Every now and then we heard a loud screeching noise above us that was being made by hornbills flying overhead. These large birds normally travelled in pairs. The sun quickly went down making the sky red and reflecting beautifully on the water of the river. Suddenly large swarms of giant-*kalongs* (fruit-bats) flew over without making a noise other than a quiet peeping noise every now and then. These bats had a wingspan of about a metre and formed a dark contrast to the red air and together with this and their reflection in the silent water of the river it gave the whole situation an unforgettable surreal effect. The people who decided to spend the night in the kampong missed all of this. It started getting dark quickly and we went to sleep. Because it was warm with no wind and we were just above the surface of the water there were thousands of mosquitoes flying around us, but I was under my mosquito net and so was not bothered by this other than the constant zooming sound. I had previously discovered that mosquitoes like the smell of dirty clothes, sweat, and especially the smell of smelly socks and went straight for them. Because of this I always placed my dirty, smelling socks close to my mosquito net in order to lure them away from me. This seemed to work quite well. The couple of mosquitoes who still managed to get inside my mosquito net could be easily caught. Though I slept quite well, throughout the night I could hear that the Papuans in the boat were constantly slapping themselves in order to kill the mosquitoes. Other than mosquitoes there were also *agoa's* (a small kind of sand fly), that could also sting you. They are so small they are able to get through the mesh of a mosquito net. Luckily they were mostly active during the day so we weren't bothered by them too much.

Sunday the 7th of June
Boat journey on the Koah river from Getenteri to Mindiptana. Float with painted Papuans. Crocodile. Measuring water depth. Boat from Mindiptana to avoid getting stranded.

We still had a long journey to go. To get from Getenteri to Mindiptana we had to go upstream on the Koah which of course took more time than going downstream on the Digoel and so we left early. The Koah is a lot narrower than the Digoel but still wider than the Mandobbo which I had been down on my last boat trip. Along the shore we frequently saw huge trees which stuck out from the rainforest. In one instance one of these trees was completely bare and covered in climbers. I never did discover whether this tree was dead or just temporarily bare. We also saw all kinds of birds flying past and a group of kalongs flew over silently, these were much smaller than the ones from the previous night at Getenteri. At one point Fred saw a large float made of tied up tree trunks which was floating down the river. On this float there was a group of brightly coloured Papuans. Fred thought that they came from far away because some were carrying bow and arrows. Based on their paintings and their jovial mood it seemed likely that they were on their way to a party. They waved and shouted at us happily. In the water there were a lot of tree trunks, often with a lot of twigs sticking out of them which our mate carefully avoided.

One of the marines discovered a crocodile in the water. It was only a small one, about 1.5 metres in length. The marine deemed it necessary to shoot at the animal, this however was not taken too kindly by the rest of the passengers.

Right at the front of the bow of our boat a good looking rooster had been tied with a piece of rope around one leg.

Along the river there were only a few kampongs. At one of these we came ashore to have a look around. As always the people were very friendly and inquisitive. It was a very neat looking kampong with bamboo houses. Here again I noticed that in the kampongs which have been under governance for a while most men wore short trousers and in some cases a vest, whereas the women still stuck to their grass skirts. Up until this point I had only seen dresses in Tanah Merah.

If the water in the Koah was low, we had the chance that our boat would get stuck in the river. At this point the water was still high, but to be sure as we reached Mindiptana the water depth was frequently checked. This was done rather primitively but effectively by tying a rock to a piece of rope and throwing it in the water in certain areas to see how far the stone sunk into the water. When, in the late afternoon we were about 20 kilometres from Mindiptana we ran into another boat, the *Sele*. This was a much smaller boat which could also reach Mindiptana when the water was low. This boat had been sent especially for us from

Mindiptana to pick up the resident in case the *Tasman* did get stuck in the water. The water level however was high enough for the *Tasman* to reach Mindiptana by evening and safely moor. The pier was made up of two levels, one for low and one for high water. When we arrived the water level was so high that the highest pier only just stuck above the water.

On the pier the head of the local government, Mr Kessler and his wife, were waiting for us. Mr Kessler was even wearing a tie for the occasion, something which was quite a strange sight in the middle of the rainforest. We kept as much to the background as possible as we were aware that these official receptions were not meant for us. First we had to walk up a wide slippery path and when we arrived at the end of this path the whole of Mindiptana was waiting for us. At the entrance of the kampong a large triumphal arch had been made with a Dutch flag in the top. Everyone had to go under this arch while we were sung to by a children's choir. The melodies were from Dutch songs, but it was Malaysian singing. We quickly came to the realisation that here we were seeing the last remnants of the Dutch colonial history.

Mindiptana turned out to be, for New Guinean standards a rather large, modern and spacious place with a lot of European looking wooden houses and an airstrip. That civilisation had reached quite far in this area could be seen by the fact that a lot of the Papuan women were wearing a, often not very clean, dress.

Our two bodyguards stayed with us, as this was their assignment. I still thought it was a strange idea that we needed bodyguards as I had still only met friendly, helpful Papuans and felt completely safe. However according to the regulations it was necessary. It did not take long before we were addressed by someone from the local government, Mr. van Diest. He asked us if we had already found a place to sleep. As it turned out we had not yet as we had been assured that there would always be room in the pasanggrahan. This was indeed the case, but Van Diest invited us to spend the night in his house. We complied to this offer and our bodyguards got a good place in the passanggrahan. We spent the evening talking to our host, and he made a remark which I remember rather well. He said that he was pleased we were not like

Commander Venema. He had been in Mindiptana not so long ago, and had also not arranged a place to sleep. He, however did not want to stay in the passanggrahan and instead insisted on having his own room with someone from the governance. Naturally this attitude was not appreciated by the locals. It seemed that Commander Venema was used to not having his say questioned in the marines and clearly did not realise that outside of this he was a civilian as well.

We also learnt that there was a usable road going from Mindiptana to Woropko. The next day we would be taken there with the only jeep in the village. Our carriers, who had left from Tanah Merah two days before, had arrived in Mindiptana already. The next day they would start walking to Woropko, this was about 50 kilometres and could be done in two days.

Because Mindiptana was the last place to send post from that we would come across for a while I had started writing more letters on the boat. It would be another two weeks until we were in Sibil, and that would be my next posting opportunity, presuming there would be a helicopter or Twin able to fly at that point, that is.

Monday the 8th of June
Jeep to Woropko. Straight growing bananas. School.

We (Fred and I) got up early because we wanted to be present when our carriers got the baggage ready to ensure nothing was forgotten. The carriers would be leaving from the church, which was stood on a small platform. When we arrived our carriers were already busy getting the baggage ready for the journey, our two body guards were also already present. After we had waved the carriers off, our host gave us a good breakfast, the last we would be having in a while. After this we walked with him to the jeep. To reach the jeep we had to walk down a slope. It was steep and slippery because it had been raining a lot, now however it was good weather. Because of the slipperiness of the road I slipped and fell almost immediately, luckily I did not hurt myself. Our jeep was ready and waiting for us. However, because of the rain from the previous night the jeep couldn't get back up the hill, and so couldn't drive to the church.

The terrain in Mindiptana wasn't as flat as in Tanah Merah. The slippery road went up and down hill and where possible over the small ridges which connected them. The ridges had the benefit that they meant water could flow to the left and right off of the road, this was very useful in an area with so much rain and the road consisted only of clay. The road was quite wide so that when the sun was shining it shone on the whole road ensuring that it would dry faster. Because our jeep was heavily loaded it sometimes had problems getting up the steep slopes because of the slippery road. When this happened we had to get out and that seemed to do the trick. On our way there were some houses here and there but we did not see any real kampongs. In one area we had to go through a small valley where a group of banana trees were stood. These were very special wild bananas because the flowers and fruit bunches were stood straight up and weren't hanging down like normal bananas. Kalkman, who had also passed this area had told me before that he had seen these as well. He thought that they may well be a new type for science. About halfway through our journey the road branched off to Ninati, the former administrative centre of the Moejoe area. There was even a real road sign at the junction, a wooden board with the word Ninati on it. After driving for about two hours we reached Woropko, where we got ourselves comfortable in the passanggrahan. The jeep drove back to Mindiptang.

That afternoon we explored Woropko. It was situated at a height of about 100 metres above sea level on slightly hilly terrain and in comparison, to Mindiptana consisted solely of bamboo houses, which looked surprisingly neat. It was only a small place, but in the area there were several kampongs and separated houses. In a lot of places there were gardens which were growing a lot of banana trees. Other than that we saw a lot of cassava and sugar cane.

Just outside of the kampong there was a very neat building which turned out to be the school. At the time that we were there, there weren't any children, but the teacher was there and he showed us the whole building. I can remember that there were some very good looking pictures on the wall of different horticultural crops. The school also had a school garden where the students each had a piece of land and learnt how best to cultivate different crops. In the kampong there was also one very tall and straight tree which was completely bare except for one green twig. This was probably a parasite or an epiphyte. High up in the same tree there was another ants nest which had a tunnel along the trunk going down, like I had seen in Hollandia-Binnen. We also had a look at a house that was still being built. Two men were busy making the floor by attaching bamboo sticks to each other with split rattan stalks.

Naturally, I was constantly on the lookout for any more mosses to add to my collection. Though this did happen, the selection of mosses wasn't very large here either. Because we were sleeping in the passanggrahan I was able to dry my collected material by placing them on the newspapers I had. Before we went to sleep we talked some more about our upcoming hike.

Tuesday the 9th of June
Woropko. A brook. Veiled lady. Carriers arrive.

We spent the whole day in and around Woropko because we had to wait for our carriers to arrive with our baggage from Mindiptana. We weren't expecting them until the end of the afternoon. According to Van der Weiden we had to take it easy today as we would need as much energy as possible for the journey still to come. Somebody had told me that there was a brook close by with moss growing around it so this is where I headed. It was an artificial stone basin on which two thin streams of water trickled through a house made of bamboo. The stones themselves were nicely covered in mosses. In part of the rainforest that was close by I also found, together with more mosses a veiled lady, a stinkhorn with a skirt. Towards the evening the carriers arrived. Their journey had been smooth and they were also offered shelter in one of the houses.

Wednesday the 10th of June
Woropko. Readying the baggage for the trek to the Sibil.

Today was a rest day, also for our carriers because the following day we would start the trek to the Sibil. Though I was looking forward to starting our journey I also felt some hesitation. I wasn't sure whether I would be able to manage the heavy journey as to I had not yet had much training. Van der Weiden told me that I should not be worried, as his experience was that the carriers often walked more slowly than we would. We did not need to carry anything whereas our Moejoe carriers had at least 20 kilos on their back.

Our carriers had started to get the baggage that they would be carrying the next day ready at the starting point next to the passanggrahan. They did not like rucksacks or harnesses, rather they bound the baggage or aluminium cans together with split rattan stalks which they bent into loops. The pack would then be carried on their back and held on by putting the loop around their head. In between the loop and the forehead, a piece of bark would often be wedged to avoid the loop cutting into their forehead. In doing this the weight was divided over their back and neck muscles which was less tiring, they also had their hands free so that they were better able to balance on wet tree trunks and the like or indeed, grab on to trees or rocks. I also prepared my own baggage.

That evening we slept in the passanggrahan, this was to be our last night's sleep in a comfortable bed for a while.

The daily course of events during the trek from Woropko to Sibil

During the trek our group always existed of, from front to back, a guide, an armed indigenous policeman, and then our carriers from the Moejoe area. Fred van der Weiden and I mostly walked along with the last group of carriers both guarded by a friendly, armed, indigenous, personal bodyguard. All the way at the back there was another armed policeman. Fred ensured that his aluminium bed was always within eyesight. Our guide not only carried baggage but also a big machete in order to cut down branches on the road. This was not often necessary as the path was frequented frequently by the locals. The police and bodyguards were forced to join us by the Dutch governance in Tanah Merah because our path went past the area of the Wambons. This tribe was not always as kindly as the Moejoes or Sibillers. This is also why all of the houses in the kampongs we passed were built on high poles: so that it was easier for the villagers to defend themselves.

The rhythm for the complete trek was about the same throughout and went as follows:

Early in the morning, about seven o'clock we were always awoken by one of our carriers, though mostly we were already awake. If there was a stream in the neighbourhood we would go there to use the toilet, wash ourselves, and clean our teeth. Our armed body guards joined us for protection. In the meantime, there was always someone who had already built a fire upon which water would be boiling for coffee. Usually, by the time we returned from the stream the coffee would be ready, sometimes we even got coffee before we went to the stream. Shortly after this breakfast was handed out, which was always made up of rice and half a can of corned beef. Our carriers received the same to eat as we did. After breakfast everyone readied their own baggage for the upcoming day and we could leave. I only had to carry a small backpack in which I had all of my camera and collecting equipment. Other than this I always carried a compass, an altimeter, iodine for disinfecting cuts, toiletries, and several kaki biscuits in case I was to get hungry. Fred too only carried several of his more personal belongings. If the group was walking too fast for us our bodyguards had to let the group know immediately, this however was never necessary. Because the policemen and bodyguards had done walks like this more often they arranged everything meaning that Fred and I did not have to worry. Up until Katem the carriers knew the area, but what was to come after was unknown territory for them as well.

The kampongs where we spent the night were always on a hill or ridge. The clay paths leading to them were often very slippery making me fall down sometimes, but there was always a carrier who helped me up. Sometimes a carrier would also fall but he too would be helped up by the others immediately. The paths in between kampongs were often hard to follow and meant that we often had to walk in mud up to our ankles and climb over thick fallen down tree trunks. Every now and then we would pass a small brook after which the path would go quite steeply down and then up again. Normally these brooks would have a slippery trunk over it. Even when crossing these trees, the carriers went to the effort to give me a hand getting over the trunk without falling into the brook even with the baggage still on their backs.

We normally left in the morning at around eight and had a break at twelve. Often one of the carriers would immediately light a fire to boil water. We were given more coffee and ate the cold rice left over from breakfast. After this we continued until about four. This is when we made camp. If there was a shelter to be found in a kampong of which the roof wasn't leaking too badly we would sleep in there. You were able to gain entrance by climbing a tree trunk with cut out steps. Fred and I would then sleep in the house with our bodyguards and several carriers and the rest would sleep under the house on the floor. Mostly though the roof would be leaking and we would have to find somewhere where it was dry. If we were unable to find anything in the kampong we would make an overhang in the woods from a big sail, we had with us. Everyone would then sleep, close together, under this sail. Our carriers always immediately started a fire in order to cook the rice and warm the cans of corned beef. In the evening tinned peas were added to the menu. During this time the carriers laughed, talked, and sang happily.

Because we spent the whole day walking through the mud our feet were always wet. We were always helped when it came to taking off the military style boots we wore. It was an honour for our carriers to be allowed to do that and it often caused a dispute as to whose turn it was, though always a very friendly one. The sewn parts of the shoes quickly started to rot and break off. Every evening we had to check whether the heel was still attached properly to the shoe. This was not always the case, which meant we had to hit the nails which kept the heel together back into place. Experience had taught us that if we did not do this the heel would need as little as a week to fall off. It was also important to get the shoes as dry as possible in the evening. The Papuans did this for us by filling the shoes up with newspapers. After a bit the newspapers would be replaced by new clean ones. Because we did not have that many newspapers at our disposal the wet ones taken out of the shoes would be re-dried in order to reuse. The shoes and socks would then be placed on a stick next to the fire. The next morning, they would be almost, mostly dry. All of our other clothes were also always wet at the end of the day, and though we tried to dry them this was not always possible due to the humidity. This meant that in the morning we had to put out wet clothes back on. When it came to putting on our shoes again we also always got help from our carriers. Often there would be two working on this at the same time, one for the right shoe and one for the left. This again was seen as an honour to do. I was happy that I had received a spare pair of boots from the marines in Tanah Merah.

After a couple of days, the journey started to get rather monotonous, though I still thought everything was great even with the rain, leeches, and mud. Especially towards the end of the day when we would make camp there was always a very cosy and fun atmosphere. The carriers knew exactly what they needed to do. Some cut down slim trees for the poles that the sail needed to hang over, others went straight into the forest in search of rattan which was split and used to tie the poles together. This all just happened and I never noticed that the Papuans had any issue or arguments with each other about it. During the trek there was no time to collect mosses as this would mess up the rhythm of the group. But during the lunch breaks and in the evening when setting up camp I still had some time to collect until it got too dark. I collected the mosses in plastic bags so that I could dry them at a later period. By this time Fred had normally already set up his aluminium bed so that he could rest and take in what was happening around him. As it turned dark everyone would be sat around the fire talking and laughing. We mostly talked about what had happened on the journey. Everyone always went to bed early as the following day there would be another long journey.

Every time we got close to a kampong the carriers started to call by making a rolling sound with their tongue, as we had noticed earlier in Sibil. This call was meant to show the villagers that there was a group of people coming with good intentions. All of the kampongs that we travelled through were rather small and messy. The houses were always stood on high poles in two rows on a ledge with a path in between. One of the poles was always a tree trunk which had been cut of rather high in order to ensure that the house was more secure. The ladder, which stuck through the floor in a square opening could be lifted up so that every house could turn into a kind of fortress. In doing so the kampongs were better able to be defended. Fred always said that the higher the poles were for the houses the more dangerous the area was. I had also heard this before from Dr. Bijkerk.

On our journey there were a lot of leeches which were especially active during the rain, which fell nearly every day. If the weather was damp and we stood still in a swampy or muddy area the leeches would immediately swarm at you and attach themselves to your ankles. To avoid the leeches climbing up my legs under my trousers I had cut of part of my trousers so that they were easier to put in my socks. Even this did not always help, and I often had them sucking at my ankles. To get them to let go we simply asked someone who was smoking a cigarette to waft the smoke in the direction of the leeches. This made them let go more easily. If you were bitten by a leech you did not really feel anything or notice it until your sock turned red with blood, and luckily they were not transmitters for any diseases. According to Fred there were less leeches off the path, so when we had a break we always did so 20-30 metres away from the path, this meant the leeches needed more time to find us.

During the whole of our journey every now and then we would hear the dim, rhythmic sound of drums. Fred said that this was done in order to let further Kampongs know that strangers were heading their way. All of the kampongs that we travelled through were empty, except for Aremko. We did not see smoke come out of a single house, as was normally the case when someone was home. It never became quite clear to me whether the kampongs were empty because of our arrival, or whether they had been empty all along, though because of the drumming that we often heard I am drawn to the first explanation.

Thursday the 11th of June
The departure. Passage over the Kaoh River to Anoemdjamdit. Flame of the Forest.

Early in the morning we (Fred and I) with our body guards and our group of Moejoe carriers were ready to go. The great adventure was about to begin. After the carriers had inspected their baggage for the last time, and had made some changes here and there, we left Woropko on the slippery path that went through the rainforest to the Kaoh River which we had to cross. After a short period of time we arrived at the shore of the river, which was still 50 to 60 metres broad in this area and way too deep to wade through. There were however three canoes ready to cross with, two of which were attached to each other. Every single journey across the river required three carriers to paddle. Because of the strong current the canoes kept floating about 40 metres away, meaning they had to be dragged back to the right place across the shore against the current. In the small canoe three carriers could be sat with their baggage, and in the double one six. This was a welcome change to walking for the carriers and they seemed to enjoy it. There was a lot of laughing especially when it seemed like something would go wrong. This seemed to happen especially with the smaller canoe, but eventually everything worked out fine. To be safer it was decided to use only the double canoe. Though we all managed to get to the other side safely doing so took us the whole morning.

When I was still in Holland people had told me that in the rainforest, especially in more open areas by rivers you could sometimes see the 'flame of the forest'. These are brightly coloured red flower clusters from the bamboo. During the whole crossing I had time to keep an eye out for them, but sadly I did not see them.[5]

---

5   I had made slides of the river and the rainforest next to it. During a slideshow in Holland someone asked what the red smudged were on the slide. It turned out that these were 'flames of the forest'. However, because I am colour blind, especially for red, I had not seen them either in the field or on the slide.

After we had crossed the river the struggle through the mud in the twilight of the forest continued. After some time, our carriers started to call out to announce our arrival at the kampong Anoemdjamdit. This kampong, like Woropko was situated at 100 metres height from the Kaoh. All in all we had only covered about 10 kilometres, but because of the time it took to cross the Kaoh it was almost four in the afternoon so we decided to spend the night here. We moved into one of the houses, which was not much more than a leaking canopy on poles. According to out carriers this shelter had been made especially for passers-by. In the inhabited houses there was no sign of smoke or fire, a sign that the kampong was (temporarily) abandoned. Because it was still relatively early I had time to look in the area for mosses. Naturally, I was joined by my bodyguard and the collected material was put into plastic sandwich bags. My experience was that it would be able to last in these for several days as long as they did not receive direct sunlight.

Friday the 12th of June
To Bian Katem and Kukubum. Big figtree. Bird of paradise.

We started our journey early. Our path seemed to be slowly going uphill and after about 15 kilometres our carriers started to call out to signal that we were getting close to the next kampong, Bian Katem. Because it was close to midday already we decided to stop here for our afternoon break. Bian Katem, which was at a height of about 200 metres was only small and existed of messily built pole houses. Here again there was not a person in sight. We spent some more time here because the next step of our journey to Kukubum was only short. This meant I had time to look for mosses, and my body guard eagerly helped me. After this we began with the last seven kilometres of the day. On our way we passed a very big tree (a *Ficus*) with dozens of set roots. Our path went over about 15 metres worth of the big system of set roots which was a new and fun experience.

At one point there was much excitement among the front group of carriers. They started calling and pointing, it appeared that they had spotted a bird of paradise who of course flew away because of the noise they were making. I was only just about to make out a brightly coloured bird with a long tail disappear into the forest.

Just before we arrived at Kukubum our carriers started calling out again and we started the slippery climb up to the kampong, which again was rather a mess and completely desolate. We did however find another canopy which was good enough for us to spend the night under. As soon as we arrived I started my search for mosses again whilst my bodyguard kept an eye on me.

Because Kukubum was situated on a hill, when stood on a certain point you could look out over the rainforest into the north. In the distance you could see a small mountain visible. This was Koereom, a small dead volcano at the foot of which Aremko, our goal for the following day, was situated. We were at this point unable to see any of the mountains behind which the Sibil Valley lay.

Saterday the 13th of June
To Aremko. 'Conversation' with a cannibal. Koreom. Foothills of the Central Mountain Range in sight.

We followed the usual ritual. After making our way through about 20 kilometres of mud in the rainforest we reached Aremko that was situated about 200 metres high on a ledge. The houses were stood on higher poles than we were used to (about four metres), a sign that fights did take place here. We found a canopy here which was also on high poles and didn't leak too much. So this is where we moved in. The kampong, was like all the others so far empty, but to our surprise after some time a man came walking towards us wearing only a nutshell. To even more surprise it turned out that he spoke several words of Dutch and Malaysian. Full of pride he showed us a smartly painted war shield which was taller and wider than he was. At the top of the shield two eyes had been painted, probably to scare the enemy. He also showed us how you used the tree trunk ladders to gain entrance to the pole houses. He tried to explain to us why he had not fled from our group. As far as we could understand he had spent a short time in prison in Hollandia because he had killed and eaten a Chinese man. Some time ago a Chinese man had come to the kampong in search of birds of paradise, in order to sell their skins for a lot of money. He was travelling by himself through the area from kampong to kampong and had a lot of baggage with him. For this baggage he hired carriers and made promises as to what they would get in return (for example rice). When it came to actually paying these people he either did not pay or did not pay enough. This had also happened in Aremko. The villagers did not appreciate this, and so they killed him. The Dutch governance heard about this and organised an expedition in search of this man. They found him and took him to prison in Hollandia. Though he was released from here quite quickly, he had managed to learn some Dutch and Malaysian.

Aremko is situated at the foot of the Koreom, a small volcano of about 50-60 metres high which we could already see from Kukubum in the distance. We asked one of the villagers whether it was possible to get to the top of the volcano. With his hands and feet he made clear that there was a path to the top and that he would take us there. According to him it was a sacred place where the patriarch of the Papuans lived. At the top there were several rocks surrounded by messy vegetation. With a lot of imagination, you were able to see a sitting figure, the patriarch of the Papuans, in the form. A lot of the trees had been cut down meaning we had a nice view of the rainforest. Though it was already rather late in the evening we were finally able to see the foothills of the Central Mountain range, behind which the Sibil Valley must be situated. We were quite happy about this because it was a sign that we were getting there. But, we still had a long way to go and the hardest path, the mountains, were still to come.

Sunday the 14th of June
To Umkubun. Ghost?

We continued our trek. The path to Umkubun rose slowly up to about 400 metres. When we arrived in the kampong it turned out that it was only very small, with a couple of empty houses on poles. There were however two shelters, without walls but with a relatively water proof roof. One of them was stood on quite tall poles and had a second floor whereas the other was on low poles without a second floor. We made our camp in the latter of the two. Several of our carriers who walked towards the front had machetes with which they could cut down overhanging plants and trees on the path. Because these machetes were a good loot for possible thieves they were always stored on the upper floors at night. This is also what we did in Umkubun, however in the night one of the heavier machetes fell through the opening in the floor into the area were part of our carriers were sleeping. One of the carriers was hit by the machete and woke up with a scream. As it was dark nobody could see what was happening. Due to the fact the carriers thought this area was haunted, everyone jumped and started making a lot of noise in an attempt to scare off the ghost. Soon enough a lamp was lit and we could see what had happened. Luckily nobody was hurt and we could continue our sleep.

Monday the 15th of June
To Oejambib. Drying the mosses.

We continued our journey to Oejambib which was situated at about 450 metres, this was the highest point of our journey over the foothills of the Central Mountain Range. We found the same here as before: an abandoned kampong which only really existed of a couple of pole houses on a clay ledge. We were unable to find any coverage here so we had to set up our own tent sail.

In the evening I installed my dry-oven. All of the mosses I had collected so far were first put into paper bags, I was helped with this by several of the Papuans. After this the bags were placed on the oven and the paraffin lamps were lit. After a couple of hours, when everyone was about to go to sleep, the mosses were almost dry. The paper bags with the mosses inside were put back into the plastic bags to ensure they would not become moist again. Because they were not quite dry yet they would have to be put back in the dry-oven when we returned to Sibil.

Tuesday the 16th of June
To Amiol.

From Oejambib we continued on to Amiol and our path descended to about 400 metres. The distance was somewhat longer than usual, about 25 kilometres, and we had to cross a lot of streams. Because the weather was rather humid there were a lot of leeches, especially in the streams we had to cross. This meant it was important to keep walking quickly as if you stood still they would all swarm towards you. Walking fast didn't avoid the fact that several leeches still managed to latch on, even in my 'anti-leech' socks. Because of the long distance we only arrived in Amiol late in the afternoon. Once again this was a very small kampong with only a few pole houses. We couldn't find any kind of shelter so we had to build our own. Because we arrived so late I did not have much time to collect very many mosses.

Wednesday the 17th of June
To Katem. Killed a snake.

Our goal for the day was Katem, that was only at about 200 metres high and at the foot of the Songgam Ravine that we would later have to go through. It was a day filled with climbing over tree trunks and wading through mud. Everyone was in a good mood because the path itself was downhill and we could look forward to a day of rest is Katem.

At one point several of the carriers started excitedly pointing and waving. The front carrier had discovered a snake of about a metre in length on the path. The snake tried to get away, but several of the carriers put down their baggage and started hitting it with sticks until it was dead. Only then were they satisfied and we could continue our journey. This was the first snake I had seen in the rainforest, but Fred assured me that though there were a lot more they fled as soon as they felt people coming, making them rather scarce. After this we walked through some secondary forest and even an alang-alang field with a rickety shelter where we decided to take out break.

Shortly after this our path became steeper and we saw the confluence of two rivers, the East-Digoel which came out of the Songgam Ravine and the Ok Iwoer. At this place there was an opening where several large tents and small huts had been built. This was Katem and it acted as a transit camp to the base camp in Sibil. The tents were made of a wooden construction of poles over which a large sail had been drawn, there were no walls. It seemed to have been washing day as in front of the tent there was a long washing line hung with clothes. The smaller buildings had leaf roofs. Close to the larger tents there were several Dutch flags hung up on high poles. We also saw a helicopter which was partially wrapped up as I had seen before in Tanah Merah. We were welcomed by police commissioner Ossterman, head of the Papuan police. We would spend the night in one of the large tents which was used for storage for all kinds of things which still needed to go to the Sibil camp by helicopter. The helicopters however were still unable to fly as it was still too overcast above the ravine.

After a week of hard graft in the rainforest a day of rest was very welcome, it also meant that we could have a lie in. This didn't really work out though as the Papuans were so used to our rhythm that the coffee was ready right on time at seven in the morning. After this I looked for some mosses in the area of the camp but did not find much. So, instead I set up the dry-oven again to finish drying the rest of my material.

In Katem there was also post ready to go to Sibil. It had already been flown by helicopter from Tanah Merah to Katem under the assumption that the flight to Sibil would be used more frequently by now. But because the helicopters were still unable to fly to Sibil the post had remained in Katem. I fished the letters that were addressed to me out of the bag together with Mr. Oosterman. There were several letters for me from home, amongst other from Hilly, mother, my brothers Jan and Gerrit, Van der Sleen, Uncle Bé and Professor van der Wijk. I did not receive anything from Uncle Wout, though I didn't expect to after his outburst from last time.

Now I also had the time to write back home and there was a good chance that the letters could be flown back to Tanah Merah. As per usual I doubt that my handwriting would have been very legible, to make it worse I did not have a table, so had to lean on my lap which probably would have made it even more difficult to decipher.

Before we went to bed we spent some time talking to Mr. Oosterman. He told us about the route through the Songgam ravine and how supplying the Sibil camp was going.

The following story is what he told us. Bär (from the geologist group) had first tried to get from Katem to the Antares by travelling past Ok Iwoer which springs from the Antaresmass. After a few days it turned out that they were not making enough progress and the helicopter was also unable to bring them more supplies so they had to return back to Katem and take the route via the Songgamravine instead. The natives path through the ravine was not used very often and had partly been overgrown again. This had been cut open again by the geologists group and in Songgam landing areas for the helicopters had been made in case they had to make an emergency landing due to the clouds. Oosterman also warned us that during our journey in the ravine we would not find any water. Along the whole route there was only one small stream which dried out if it did not rain for a few days. The only other way to get water then was to squeeze out the moss pollen. We also heard that since the 29th of April there had not been another flight to Sibil.

After this conversation Fred and I continued talking about our previous journey and what was still awaiting us.

Friday the 19th of June
Through the Songgam Ravine to Songgam and Ariemkop. Rattan bridges. Cut on finger 'treated' by carrier. Found the clearing and brook by Songgam. Heard a helicopter.

Today we started our last, but also most gruelling, part of the journey to the base camp. We had to travel through the narrow Songgam Ravine via Songgam and Ariemkop to Sibil. The aim was to finish this trek of about 40 kilometres in two days. The trip was also more exciting for our Moejoe carriers now because they were unfamiliar with the area too.

As soon as we left Katem we had to travel over the Ok Iwoer. This river was not very wide but was fast flowing and full of rocks and pebbles. Because of this we could not wade over or use canoes. Instead the Papuans had built a bridge from rattan over the river. On both sides of the river there was a kind of ladder made against a tree trunk. Between both tree trunks there were three strands of plaited rattan strung over the river. The idea was that you walked over the bottom strand. Above this were the two other strands which you could hold on to. The three strands were also connected by vertical threads of rattan. There were quite a lot of these vertical connections which were broken. Before we could go over the bridge the breaks needed to be fixed. A couple of our carriers did this with a lot of enthusiasm while the rest shouted, laughed, and encouraged them. After about half an hour it was decided that the bridge was safe enough for us to cross and the first carrier went across, encouraged by the rest of the group. After this the rest of the carriers went over one by one and we followed last with the body guards. We had been warned to try to not look down, of course this didn't work as for every step you had to look down to see where you put your foot. So I did look down, and suddenly it was as if the river was stood still and I, together with the bridge was soaring at a tremendous speed above the water. This was a very strange sensation and if I shut my eyes and opened them again whilst looking forward everything went back to normal. This process repeated itself several times before I crossed the river. The reason that we went over the bridge one by one was because of the weight but also because of how violently the bridge swung when walking over it. If we were to go over two at a time this may have worsened. After we had crossed the river we continued on the path, soon enough we arrived at the East-Digoel which we also had to cross. This river was a lot broader than the Ok Iwoer and just as fast flowing. The local Papuans had also built a bridge over this river although longer. This bridge was in better state than the last and didn't need as much work. The crossing happened much the same as the last, with a lot of happy excitement and laughing. Because this bridge was longer the flying sensation that I had experienced also happened more often. You could also tell this by the carriers, if they suddenly gripped hold of the sides, stared straight ahead, and stood still only to continue normally later on you knew they had just experienced the same thing.

Straight after we had crossed the second bridge we slowly started to go up hill. The path that had been hacked out by the geologists didn't go down through the ravine along the East-Digoel but higher along the steep West slope.

After climbing slowly for several hours we arrived in a karst area with erratically shaped limestone. The path here had a lot of potholes mixed with sharp edged stones. This meant that we had to be especially careful not to fall. I still ended up nearly falling once, but luckily I managed to grab on to a rock. This however led me to cutting myself on my finger which started to bleed quite badly. One of the carriers saw that I was bleeding, took my finger and put it in his mouth! He sucked the blood up, spat it out, then put my finger back in his mouth and massaged the wound for about ten minutes with his tongue. When he took my finger out of his mouth he told us that everything was fine again and that I would not get an infection. This turned out to be true. After we stuck a plaster on the wound we continued our journey.

The area that we were trekking through became very dry because all the rain water went straight into the limestone. There was not a brook or puddle of water in sight which was very unusual for us. After some time the woods became more moist and opened up. At one point we saw the clearing that the geologists had created for the helicopters to make an emergency landing due to weather circumstances. The clearing was situated in a small area of cut down forest and was about six by six metres where the helicopter could land. The platform, that was made of trunks from the cut down trees was a good place for us to take a break. The area of the clearing had been selected well as close by we found the stream that Mr. Oosterman had told us about. It was only a very thin trickle of water that came out of the rock, but enough to fill our canteens meaning there was no need to squeeze out moss pollen. I am not sure whether this stream was part of the underground river system of the Sibil River.

As an exception to the rule it was a dry day without many clouds which meant that we had great views over the ravine with the steep and wooded slopes. We were only just at the entrance of the ravine at about 500 metres high and we still needed to get up to the kampong Ariemkop at about 1000 metres height. In some places we were able to look through the trees into the ravine and we could see how steep it was and how deep. We were looking into the ravine at about 700 metres where the Digoel should be flowing at about 300 metres. The river itself could however not be seen because of the forest, but we could hear it. If we looked up along the ravine we could see that the mountains were a lot higher. We had to go over these mountains, we still had a long way to go.

At one point, below us in the valley we could hear the sound of a helicopter. We couldn't see the helicopter because of the trees, but we could hear that the sound moved away from us in the direction of the Sibil camp. Shortly after this we heard the helicopter return in the direction of Katem. Later we heard that the helicopter had made several trips that day.

During a long break in the Songgam I was able to collect some mosses in the area of the clearing. After this we continued our journey to Ariemkop which was at about 1000 metres high. The distance we still needed to go wasn't very great but the path was rather steep meaning we didn't arrive until rather late in the day and I was unable to do any collecting.

We had noticed that we no longer had any problems with the leeches as we normally did. We assumed that this was probably because we had climbed so high there were no longer part of the environment.

In Songgam as well as Ariemkop we had not seen any houses, meaning we had to set up our own camp again. Our carriers were now well practiced in doing so it didn't take very long to do. It started getting dark quite quickly, but the cosy fire with the rice pot above it provided enough light. It had been a tiring day but everyone seemed happy and satisfied. The goal of our journey, the Sibil camp, was fast approaching and because we had travelled further today, tomorrow would be easier.

Saturday the 20th of June
To the base camp. Lost. Jááááp. Skin painted white? Pointed in the right direction of Mabilabol. Toeloe.

We were awoken again by our carriers at seven in the morning with coffee and breakfast (as per usual rice and corned beef). Fred van der Weiden wanted to stay in his aluminium bed for an extra hour because we didn't have that far to walk anymore. The carriers, however, preferred to leave at the normal time (8 o'clock). Thus the agreement was made that the group would split up. Most of the carriers were to leave at the normal time, and we would stay behind with some carriers, our body guards, and of course Fred's bed. We would then set off at around ten in the morning.

The path continued up hill, which was no surprise as where we left off in the morning was at about 1000 metres high and the base camp was at 1300 metres. However, we continued up and up, at first we were not concerned as we thought we had to go over another mountain ridge. However, our altimeter was showing a reading of 2000 metres which made us start to doubt whether we had followed the right trail. After discussing this with the carriers we came to the conclusion that we were lost. Fred wasn't worried at all however, as he had experienced things like this more often. We were on a mountainside on which the woods was rather thin and low in some places meaning you were able to look into the valley. In the depths of the valley we could see small plumes of smoke rising. "Where there is smoke there is fire, and where there is fire there are people" said Fred and so we decided to step off of the path and instead walk headfirst into the direction of the smoke through the woody thicket. One of the carriers went in front with a big machete that we had with us, he used the machete to create a path through the thicket and straight to the smoke. After about half an hour of going downhill at some speed we arrived at the source of the smoke and saw that it was coming from a single hut. Everything was of course deserted as the inhabitants would have heard us coming a long time ago and hidden in the woods to be safe. We decided to wait outside of the hut until someone showed up. This didn't take very long as the locals were of course also rather curious. To start off with we heard some twigs break and then we saw two eyes looking at us from behind a tree. A litter later a boy came out to us followed by a man and another boy. As per usual we offered them some kaki's. We had to show them that they could be eaten first and as soon as they realised this they started eating the kaki's themselves as well. They were very excited and the two boys came up to me and started stroking my hands, arms, shoulders, and head and shouting out 'Jááááp'. We already knew from our visit to Koekding that his meant something like 'pretty' or 'nice'. At one point the man came up to me, grabbed my hand spat into it and started rubbing it heavily. Later I learnt that Papuans who have never met white people before do this in order to see whether we hadn't just been painted white. When they were done with this ceremony they let loose another 'Jááááp', it seemed that they were now convinced that my skin really was white and that they were rather pleased with this result. They didn't do the same to Fred as he is half Indonesian and so his skin wasn't as light.

When they had quietened down we started calling out: 'Mabilabol, Mabilabol.' We knew that this was the Papuan name for the area where our base camp had been built. They copied what we said and based on their body language you could tell that they knew that we wanted to go there. After this the man said something to us which we didn't understand and he walked away leaving the two boys behind. After about fifteen minutes he came back joined by his wife and a daughter. The woman had a load of fire wood on her back. She greeted us in a friendly way and disappeared into the hut. The man also went into the hut but came out again straight away with his bow and arrow. He made clear to us that we should follow him and the boys, we followed him over a rather easy path. After about half an hour we came to a fork in the path and he made clear to us through shouting 'Mabilabol' that we should take the path which headed downwards. We then said goodbye to him and the boys with the knuckle greeting and descended onto the right path. It didn't take long before we reached an area with a wonderful view over the Sibil Valley and we could see the camp and the air strip lying within it. It was only now that we realised how high we had really climbed, which would have been unnecessary if we had simply followed the right path. After descending even more, we reached another kampong which we later realised must have been Toelo. The people from this kampong often came to the base camp and some of our expedition members had also travelled to this kampong themselves. The result of this was that the villagers were not at all surprised when we arrived and that none of the fled into the forest.

Toelo was only a small kampong and built the same as Betabib: a round square with a low fence made of twigs. There were four houses outside the square where the people lived and two houses inside the square. One of these houses was the iwool (sacred man's house), I do not know what the function of the other one was. There had been several jaws of pigs attached to the outside of the iwool. We were greeted in a very friendly manner by all of the villagers, men, women and children. It was clear that the villagers were already used to white people because they did not start stroking us. The women and children also did not keep to the back, as often happened when they were not sure who or what we were. We could not stay here very long because it was already rather late.

The further descent into the base camp went through rainforest in which in some places the undergrowth was so thick we had to crawl under it. Just before we arrived in the base camp we still had to wade knee deep through the Sibil. Naturally we were greeted heartily by all of the people at the base camp including my friends from before. The other carriers had arrived somewhere around eleven and since we only arrived in the late afternoon it was rather clear that we had taken rather a large detour.

When Dr. Romeijn and the marine doctor Tissing heard that I was back they wanted to see me immediately in order to check for themselves whether my leg had healed properly and whether or not I was allowed to walk again. After they had thoroughly checked the wound I was given permission to walk again. I was, however, told off for walking for nearly two weeks straight through the rainforest without their consent.

The chief Venema who I had also met in Tanah Merah had arrived the previous day by helicopter in the Sibil meaning we could meet each other again. I was also heard that the food shortage issues had improved greatly as on the fifth of June there had been a food drop done by the Dakota. To add to this the helicopters were now also able to fly to the base camp. This lead to there being much optimism concerning the possibilities of climbing the Antares rather soon.

Behind the Silver House a big sail had been hung up where the hundred carriers of the land registry had their shelter. Fred also slept there in his own aluminium bed. We ate some dried out rice with corned beef and after this I went to bed early in my trusted bed of jute bags.

Sunday the 21st of June
Base camp. Collecting and photo-material arrived in Sibil. Lucky with the leg injury.

I heard that on the day that we were trekking through the Songgam Ravine (19th of June) the helicopter was able to fly back and forth from Katem to the base camp seven times because of the nice weather. Funnily enough we had only heard the helicopter twice. This was probably because we were walking high above the river through the ravine and the helicopter was flying much lower.

All of my missing items had now arrived in Sibil by helicopter. The dry-oven I had brought with me myself, and the ballpoints had also arrived from Holland. I was most happy with the fact that after being sent all over the place my film rolls had finally arrived by helicopter.

The rest of the day I spent drying the rest of the rather large collection of mosses I had collected during the journey.

I was told that the geologist group had created six clearings between Sibil and Katem. I was rather surprised by this and the fact that we had only come across one on our own journey. This meant that the geologist group had taken a different route than I had with the cadastre group. I presume that we were walking higher along the slope as we could hear the helicopter flying beneath us. This also meant that there were more paths than we were aware of. This had also been shown on the last day when we got lost. We had seen forks in the road up to 2000 metres high where we sometimes weren't sure which one to take.

Wim Vervoort told me that due to the initiative of Jaap Reynders, by the biologist group (Wim Vervoort, John Staat and Cees van Heijningen) including Jaap Reynders and Alfred van Sprang a trip had been made of 10 days (18th until 28th of May) to Tenmasigin and the Ok Tenma (Orion Mountains.)

It was my understanding that the other members of the biologist group had not been able to do much up until now, other than the journey to the Orion Mountains. This was due to the fact that there was not any collecting or prep material available. It was because of this information that I realised that I had not missed much, and that I had probably been rather lucky with my leg injury. If this had not happened I would have missed out on my stay in Tanah Merah and of course the whole journey back to the Sibil. Instead I had gained great insight and oversight into the moss vegetation in the lowland rainforest up to about 1300 metres.

From the Silver House I still often heard Brongersma's typewriter rattling while he worked on his journal or his book *The White Heart of New Guinea* with a cigarette dangling in the corner of his mouth. I was given a strong impression that Venama's part in the book may well be rather small as I never saw or heard him type anything. Brongersma and Venema still played a lot of patience together. But some things had changed. Brongersma no longer read the *Panorama* but *de Spiegel* and Venema had gone from *Panorama* to a detective novel. Flip, Jan Sneep's dog, had a girlfriend now. It was these 'changes' that I put down as the most important events in the camp while I was away in my letters home. This rather illustrates how in the month and a half that I was gone hardly anything had happened. This was all due to the delay regarding the receiving of material, something which Brongersma could not help either. There was some hope however that because the two helicopters had now been in the Sibil they would soon be able to start supplying bivouac 39 at the foot of the Antares.

Monday the 22nd of June
Base camp. Back to Betabib. Looking in a iwool.

My two friends joined me early. I thought it would be fun to visit Betabib again, this was the kampong closest to our base camp and I had been there before. It seemed that since that time nothing had changed. The two village elders Bomdogi and Wasonim were sat, like the first time, on the floor in the middle of the central square.

We were greeted as friends with the knuckle greeting. My friends came up with the idea that I should also take a look in the iwool stood in the middle of the square. Of course I was also curious about what one would see in an iwool. So we asked the elders (with our hands and feet) whether we would also be allowed to take a look in the iwool. I noticed that this question causes some shyness to come over them. They started talking together in heavy voices and kept pointing at my beard. From what I understood they were convinced that I was a man because of my beard and because of this could not deny me entry into the iwool. After a short while I was invited to take a look. Wasonim went over a shaky tree trunk onto the even more rickety deck and took the sticks and plank away from the door opening (which was more a window). He went inside and waved me on to follow him. He must have realised that it would not be as easy for me to get over the shaky log so he put his hand out to help me over and avoid me falling. Bomdogi also joined us inside. On the inside it was rather dark, and like most of the houses it only consisted of a hearth. During the visit there was lively talk and gesturing. I happily talked back to them in Dutch as I did not want to give them the impression that I could not talk. Afterwards, satisfied and an experience richer we walked back to the camp together.

Tuesday the 23rd of June
Area around the base camp. Cadastre group left with Verstappen and Nicolas on foot to Antares.

During my first stay in the camp I had collected quite a few samples. However, a lot of them I was not able to dry properly and these had gone mouldy. There were also some samples which I had accidentally set fire to while trying to find a way to dry them. A lot of them needed to be collected again because of this. This was rather easy as mosses, and to a lesser extent also lichens, grew everywhere in great amounts. Because my dry-oven was now here I was able to dry the new samples rather easily. So I continued to busily collect the mosses, and was of course helped in this by my two friends.

Every now and then I heard the helicopters flying who had started to transport materials and food to bivouac 39 at the foot of the Antares. The cadastre group (Van der Weiden with 50 Moejoe carriers) and Verstappen, Escher and Lieutenant Nicolas, went via bivouac 36 on foot to bivouac 39 at 1300 metres at the foot of the Antares. It was from this point that the climb would start.

There was good hope that the climb of the Antares, one of the main goals of this expedition would finally be possible.

After the official beginning of the expedition on the 10th of April about two and a half months had gone by in which I, as well as the rest of the biologist group had been able to do relatively little in the Sibil. Only Tanah Merah and the journey to the Sibil had provided me with some results. Other than the rather long wait in Hollandia and Tanah Merah I was enjoying myself immensely. Professor Lam had already warned me that these kinds of things may happen.

Wednesday the 24th of June
Base camp. Helicopters supply bivouac 39. Making collections ready for shipping.

The sun was shining again and it seems like suitable weather to continue supplying bivouac 39. Early in the morning we heard the helicopter rise high above the airstrip. The pilot, Warman, did this so that he could see whether the Orion Mountains and the valleys of the Ok Tsjop and Ok Bon were cloudless, then he could continue his mission to supply bivouac 39. It appeared that this was indeed the case and, that day, five trips were made to bivouac 39 and another two to bivouac 36, which was situated half way between the base camp and the bivouac by the Antares. As bivouac 39, from where the climbing of the Antares would start, had been completed it would not be long until we could really get started. The aim was for the biologists leave for bivouac 39 on the 26th of June via helicopter. It seemed I had arrived right in time from Tanah Merah.

The Twin was supposed to come in the next day and the air strip was in good order, so there was a big chance that all of the material I had collected during my trip to the base camp and the surrounding areas would be able be sent to Hollandia in order to be sent back to Holland from there. This meant I had my work cut out for me.

To make the samples ready to post, the collections of mosses in plastic bags were put into bigger plastic bags or cardboard boxes, which were then put into larger boxes again. The boxes were sealed with waterproof tar paper and the seams covered with a thick band of plastic tape. Great emphasis had been put on how expensive this tape was and that we had to be very careful not to use more than absolutely necessary, so much so that we hardly dared use it. We had also been asked to reuse the tape if it had been used on a smooth surface. The boxes all got their own label with the contents and the address. All of the mosses were packaged up with the other collected materials in wooden chests and sent to Leiden. Here the moss samples would be split. A full set of duplicates would then be sent to Groningen in order for them to work on identifying, separating and naming the collection.

Thursday the 25th of June
Twin brings post and takes collected materials back to Hollandia.

It was highly likely that the biologist group would be heading to the Antares by helicopter the next day and so it was high time to start collecting and readying all the things we needed. For me this was the dry-oven, the hurricane lamps, and the petroleum needed for them. Other than that I needed: plastic bags, lots of paper bags, labels, field notebook, writing equipment, photo material and so on. All of the things I needed to bring with me (except the dry-oven) was put into big plastic bags so that everything would stay dry. Of course I also needed clean clothes.

Though it was rather cloudy in Sibil the Twin was still able to land as the pilot had found a gap in the clouds just above the camp. The post for the expedition members which had been in Hollandia, Tanah Merah, and Mindiptana a couple of weeks ago was brought by Twin. Other than this there was also post from other outposts. The Twin took our post and all of the material we had collected so far back to Hollandia in order to send it on to Holland.

We heard that Alfred van Sprang had already flown from bivouac 36 to bivouac 39 on the foot of the Antares to see what progress had been made for the geologist who were supposed to create the path to the top of the Antares, but they were still in bivouac 36.

Friday the 26th of June
The approach to climbing the Antares. Taking the helicopter to bivouac 39. Papuans with mercantilism.

One of the most important goals of the expedition was to climb the Antares, the highest top of the Star Mountains. The mountain had never been climbed before. The Papuans had never climbed it either because they believed there were angry spirits living in the higher mountains who, if disturbed, would take out their anger on the climbers. This meant that a path to the top still needed to be created. According to old estimates the Antares was about 4000 metres high. After studying aerial photos, a point had been chosen on the Ok Bon close to the confluence with the Ok Minam as a starting point for the climb. A group, led by the geologist Escher, had made a path of about 15 kilometres from bivouac 36 to the foot of the Antares and built bivouac 39 here. Based on the aerial photos one could see that between Ok Bon and Ok Minam, which both originate from the Antares mass, a small mountain ridge went up to the highest ridge of the mass and then further to the highest top. This would then also be the route for the climb. The idea was that the geologists, Herman Verstappen and Arthur Escher, with the marine lieutenant Nicolas and a group of carriers would leave from bivouac 39 and climb the Antares first, to cut a path to the top and create a small bivouac (no. 40) about half way up. Bivouac 39 had been fully supplied by helicopter from the base camp in the last couple of days. The biologist group would then climb the Antares upon return of the geologist group via the created path.

Now the big day had finally come, the climb of the Antares could start. It was going to get busy in bivouac 39. The geologist group, led by Escher, was already present and the cadastre group, led by Van der Weiden, was also on their way by foot. Verstappen and Nicolas had joined the cadastre group. The aim for the cadastre group was to do an exact location determination. Other than this the journalists Alfred van Sprang (from *de Spiegel*) and Klaarenbeek (from *het Parool*) had also already arrived in bivouac 39. The biologist group consisting of Cees van Heijningen, Cees Kalkman, John Staats, Wim Vervoort, and myself would be flown one by one with our personal baggage by helicopter to bivouac 39.

Brongersma had asked Wim Vervoort, as the oldest of the group, to act as the leader in the period of time we would spend on the Antares.

The helicopters had to fly a height of more than 2000 metres, which meant only one passenger, with their baggage, could be taken each trip. To reduce the weight of the helicopter even more the pilot (Mr. Warman) had taken both doors off. I would be the last of my group to fly to bivouac 39. Luckily, the weather stayed good so that all of the planned flights were able to take place. Though, as usual, clouds built up above the mountains in the afternoon, Warman still dared to take the last flight of the day. My baggage was tied to the floats of the helicopter and I got in. Because there were no doors I was fastened in by Warman with two broad belts. He told me that if I wanted to I could hang out of the door to take pictures during the flight. This was going to be my first helicopter flight. Straight after take-off I got a good oversight of the barracks in our camp and soon we were flying over the flanks of the Orion Mountains. This is when the true rugged nature of the mountains became evident. My earlier flights with the Dakota from Sentani to Merauke had shown me some indication of this but because we were flying lower now everything was much clearer. All of the mountainsides were forested, but to my surprise in front of us I saw a large area of mountainside which was empty. From a distance it looked like the aftermath of a big landslide but, as we got closer I saw houses on the slope. It seemed to be that the empty parts were gardens, surrounded by the faintly visible fences. Though the visibility was still good, above the mountain ridges more and more clouds were gathering. Shortly after this I saw the steep and deep valley of the Ok Tsjop, which Herberts had told me about before. After this we descended and flew into the steep and deep valley of the Ok Bon. A thick cloud front had floated over but luckily it did not descend into the valley so we were able to fly under it until we reached bivouac 39. I knew the geologists had built several platforms for the helicopter to land, in different locations, in case of an emergency. However, I was unable to see these clearings from the air. I did see the low slopes of the Ok Bon and several small kampongs which consisted of only several houses, here again you could spot several fenced gardens.

When our helicopter landed on the platform at bivouac 39 we were not only welcomed by the people living in the bivouac, but also by the local Papuans. It seemed that there were one or more kampongs in the neighbourhood.

In order to avoid getting trapped by the clouds Warman decided to fly back to the base camp straight away. I met the geologist Escher, for the first time, who until recently had been the only inhabitant of this bivouac. I had met the others before, either in the basecamp or in Hollandia.

Bivouac 39 was situated at 1300 metres on the Ok Bon on a small horizontal piece of land close to the confluence with the Ok Minam. This was the only flat area suitable for building the bivouac on. The first river sprang from the highest top of the Antares and the other from the West top. Both rivers were still small and easy to wade through at this point. The bivouac consisted of a platform for the helicopters and a big sail with a floor on low poles to ward off vermin and possible high water. A smaller shelter at the back of ours had been made for our carriers. A bridge had already been made over the Ok Bon from tree trunks and with a railing. A couple of the carriers were busy collecting more tree trunks in order to repair the bridge in case it became damaged by high water.

It was still rather early in the afternoon so there was still time to explore the area and collect some samples. The trees previously on the slopes by the bivouac had been cut down in the past so it mostly consisted of low secondary bush and was rather a mess. A little higher on the slop there was still some rainforest. There were not very many well developed mosses. You could clearly tell by the vegetation by the stream that it had recently flooded. Between the plants on the shore there was still a thin layer of silt. This did not stop the grasses from growing here and there, including puzzlegrass and a little further from the shore also blooming touch-me-not's (*Impatiens*) were growing.

Along the shore there were several decaying trunks, a sign that the now peaceful stream could become so rough that it could carry tree trunks with it. The carriers used one of these trunks as a place to sit.

The zoologists, when gathering animals in the area, were helped greatly by the local Papuans. By making gestures, and using some of the words we had already learnt we were able to make clear what animals we were talking about. At first they looked at us as if we were crazy and trying to convince them of strange things. As soon as they saw that we really did reward them with mirrors and matches they quickly started showing up with all kinds of insects and lizards. I have no doubt that at times they will have struggled with their options; either eating the insect or giving it to us for a reward.

Some of the Papuans were rather mercantilist. If someone had for example caught ten lizards, he would first show five and receive a mirror for that, after which he would show the other five and also want a mirror for them. Within a very short amount of time the price for a lizard had risen tremendously. When they did not think they were getting enough of a reward they would simply let the animals go again.

At that time, I had not found very many mosses, and so it was not viable to put the dry-oven on. The collected mosses were instead packaged in order to take with me to bivouac 39A.

It had been an interesting and busy day and in the evening, by the light of a hurricane lamp we talked about the experiences of the day. We had to be frugal with the use of petroleum and before long the light was turned off and everyone went to sleep in our new home. Later in the night it started to rain which caused the noise of the stream to increase.

Saturday the 27th of June
Geologist and cadastre group go to bivouac 39A with Van der Weiden. Biologist group goes to bivouac 39A and back to 39.

The previous night it had continuously rained but at sun up it became clear again. The murmur of the brook had turned into a wild roaring. It was simply not possible for our bivouac to be built much higher than the water level and for a moment I was worried whether we would actually stay dry. Luckily, the bivouac had been built on poles high enough to skirt the water. That morning it appeared that the Ok Bon had risen quite a bit and the bridge over it had been partially torn down. Several of the Papuans were already busy fixing it. The materials they had readied the day before were of good use now.

Shortly before we arrived in bivouac 39 Arthur Escher had already explored the western slopes of the Antares mass. The biologists climbed the steep path, which went through a very messy secondary forest with a lot of bamboo. It appeared that in the past the Papuans had already cut and burnt this area. This was evident from the thick, burnt trunk lying on the slope. The trunk was completely covered with an encapsulating *Hypnodendron*, a big moss type which looks like a small tree. Another burnt trunk was covered with some kind of Turkey Tail (fungus). On the slope I also found the young buds of a *Balanophora*, a root parasite. After we climbed for about 250 metres we came through a screw pine (*Pandanus*) wood. After this the path that Escher and his group had cut descended by about 40 metres to a basin in the slope in which a marsh had developed with a lot of grass, sphagnum, and bulrush. This marsh was almost completely dried out and there was only a small puddle of water. Along the marsh there was a narrow ridge at about a height of 10 metres. Earlier Escher had started to create a new bivouac. This place was a lot more appropriate for a longer stay than the location of bivouac 39, in the narrow valley of Ok Bon.

Our Moejoes were still working hard building the new bivouac. With surprise I watched them at work; it happened very efficiently. Some of the Papuans went into the forest to collect rattan which grew everywhere in the screw pine wood. These rattan stems were carefully cleaved and put in a pile. Others cut down thin straight tree trunks which were also plentiful along the outskirts of the marsh. The rest was busy creating wooden structures and tying it up with the split rattan. Everything happened extremely quickly and efficiently amidst a lot of talking and laughing. Fred kept a close eye on the whole of the 'building project' and gave some instructions every now and then.

Originally it had not been planned to build a bivouac by the marsh so it still needed to be given a number. We couldn't give the bivouac a higher number because these names had already been given to the other bivouac's which were going to be built higher up the mountain. There were two options: 'bivouac 39bis' and 'bivouac 39A'. After some discussion we settled on calling the new bivouac 39A.

The research facility had largely been finished already. I was extremely impressed by the fact that the Papuans were able to build to these standards in only a matter of days. A canopy, for the carriers, had also been put together with sail. They were still working on the 'kitchen' which was made of a hearth on the ground and a leaf canopy. A lot of fire wood had already been gathered however. Work was also still ongoing building a ladder of about 10 metres high from the marsh to the camp. Another thing which was still being built was the toilet, this would be a very steep ladder with a platform which overhung the lower valley of the Ok Minam, 200 metres below. This toilet was not a success as the slope was so steep and the drop so deep that no one dared to use it. Instead a piece of woods a little way from the camp was assigned to be the 'toilet woods'. Closer to the camp we agreed to a place we could pee. A lot of fruit fly-like flies were attracted to this area because of the salt.

I was able to collect quite a lot of samples in and around bivouac 39A. After this we returned, satisfied, to bivouac 39.

Sunday the 28th of June
To bivouac 39A. Geologists leave for the top of that Antares.

Bivouac 39A had been finished off enough for us to move in. To save on food some of the Moejoe carriers were sent back to the base camp. All of our belongings and equipment were taken to the new camp by the remaining Moejoes and some of the more local Papauns. Most of the inhabitants of bivouac 39 were now going to move into the newly built bivouac 39A. Wim Vervoort decided to stay in bivouac 39 for a while longer in order to do more collecting. With the help of the Papuans he would be able to collect a lot more animals from the valley of the Ok Bon and the Ok Minam. Kalkman and Brandenburg van den Gronden (marine) also decided to stay in bivouac 39 a while longer. Other than the geologist- and biologist group two reporters (Van Sprang and Klaarenbeek), several marines and several native police men would be joining us to bivouac 39A. Only one marine and a handful of Moejoe carriers stayed in bivouac 39 in order to provide protection.

For the climb to bivouac 39A we followed the same steep path we had followed the day before. Our most important equipment, so my dry-oven and petroleum was carried up by the carriers. As per usual I was only carrying a small rucksack with my collection material, photography equipment, and some biscuits.

During the climb I was still able to collect some mosses which I had not seen before.

When we arrived in bivouac 39A the geologist group which had left bivouac 39 the day before were still getting ready to leave for the climb up the Antares. The group was made up of the geologists Verstappen and Escher, and the lieutenant of the marines, Nicolas. Six carriers would be joining them, as well as twenty carriers from the cadastre group. The six carriers would continue the journey completely with the climbers and the twenty carriers from the cadastre group would, after dropping their luggage off at bivouac 40, immediately return to bivouac 39A.

The plan was that the group would be back in bivouac 39A in seven days. Because of this they brought seven days' worth of food and some extra in case of delays or emergencies. On their journey, on the ridge that they had to climb over, water would most likely be scarce and they brought two jerry cans of water with them from the pool at bivouac 39A. the climbers were waved off as they crossed the dry marsh. The weather was still dry and we could see their aluminium carrying tins shining for a long time in the dark wood, until the group disappeared into the forest on the way to the ridge, over which they would be able to climb to the top of the mountain.

The biologist group would stay in bivouac 39A until the geologists returned. After this our biologist group would also head up the mountain to do research.

It was still good weather which meant that we were able to spend the afternoon collecting. Above the march, especially close to the pool, there were plenty of insects. This meant that the zoologists were very busy waving their nets around, trying to catch them, and catch them they did!

Now, I also had the time to explore and investigate the marsh more thoroughly. It was a very idyllic place, completely surrounded by rainforest. I estimate that the actual marsh probably had a diameter of 300 metres. At the edges it slowly changed into bush and then into the high jungle. Due to the dry weather you could walk through it without getting wet feet. The floor vegetation consisted mostly of grasses, bulrushes and in several places a sphagnum moss species.[6] The bushy vegetation around the edge of the marsh was incredibly rich with mosses, liverworts, orchids, ferns, lichens and all kinds of other things. What I noticed the most was the colour of the vegetation. Anywhere where the sun could reach, the mosses were a brown to deep purple or almost black colour. This applied to the kinds on the floor, but also those growing on twigs or trunks. The brown colour was mostly caused by the immense amount of large pollen from the liverwort *Chandonanthus* and the moss genus *Macromitrium*. The purple or almost black colour was mostly caused by the large clusters of different kinds of the liverwort genus *Frullania*. Everywhere there were metre long strands of mosses (like *Floribundaria*) hanging from the trees. The leaves of most of the bushes also had a red tinge to them. All of these colours stood in stark contrast to the uniform green colour which normally existed in the rainforest, as in most places there was no direct sunlight. The amount of different kinds of small flowered orchids was also rather noticeable. The orchids grew everywhere, on the floor, on the tree trunks, or in the centre of mosses. It was often easier to spot ten different kinds of orchids than ten of the same species. I also saw an arum as tall as a man which was about to flower. The area around us was so rich in species that I could have collected mosses and liverworts unknown to science every single day, for many days.

To me, the best thing about this paradise was the sheer diversity of plants and animals that had been created by nature. People had had no influence on any of it, and this area had never been seen before.

Towards the end of the afternoon the cadastre carriers arrived back at bivouac 39A. They had taken their load to bivouac 40 (2400 metres high) and had come back in order to save on supplies.

In the evening I was very busy sorting, labelling, and drying all of the mosses I had collected at bivouac 39 and 39A. This was done by the bright light of a Tilley lamp. Lighting the Tilley lamp was not so easy,

---

6 Later investigation upon my return home showed that this sphagnum species was new for science. I described the moss as *Sphagnum antarense* Zanten & Wijk spec. nov.

especially not when a new wick was needed. We had a special person to do this. After this I used my dry-oven to dry all of the mosses. This happened under the canopy at the entrance of our accommodation.

Monday the 29th of June
Organization of bivouac 39A.

The bivouac stood about 20 metres above the dried up marsh on a narrow, 15-metre-wide ridge between the marsh and Ok Minam. The back of our accommodation directly adjoined to the sheer 200 metre drop to the Ok Minam and at the front there was a steep slope down to the marsh. On this slope there was a slippery 'path' which had been made to the entrance of our bivouac, made of dugout steps, tree trunks, and several short improvised pieces of ladder. It was quite an art to get up without falling over, which happened quite often. The roof was, like bivouac 39, a big sail. At the entrance a canopy of leaves had been made. Because it rained so frequently the roof often began to leak and we were always having to repair it. The canopy helped to make sure that the rain didn't come in.

Our house was a sleeping room, eating room, workroom, and a storage room. There was a path in the middle with, on one side all of the sleeping areas with the camp beds, and on the other side tables, which were used to work at as well as to eat and drink coffee. In the front area I had set up my dry-oven carefully so that the mosses would not be hit by the raindrops leaking through. It was always a cosy place to be, especially in the evening when everyone was home and doing their thing.

My sleeping place was right at the back of our accommodation next to the abyss. There was no wall separating me from the drop down to the valley floor, so I had to make sure that I didn't turn around too much in my sleep in order to avoid falling into the Ok Minam. When I wanted to crawl into bed I discovered that there were several green tree frogs which had climbed under my mosquito net and into my bed. It seemed they gained entrance into our house along the poles it stood on. I caught them before I went to sleep and gave them to the zoologists. The Tilley lamp was always turned off rather early and everything went pitch black. During the night we heard some excitement coming from the canopy, under which the carriers slept. We didn't pay much attention to it.

As normal during both day and night there was not a lot of wind. During the night however, I heard a fall wind on the opposite side of the Ok Minam rolling down several times. A fall wind occurred on clear nights as the air cooled down at the top of the mountain. It then rolled, in pockets, down the slope. The fall wind started high by the West top of the Antares and ended in the 2000 metre lower valley of the Ok Minam. As I slept at the edge of our accommodation, without walls, I was able to hear the fall winds rather well. On later nights I did not hear it because it stayed cloudy, which meant that the air on the mountain top cooled down less.

We were hopeful that we would now be able to reach the top of the Antares and we named the bivouac 'Huize de Goede Hoop' (House of Good Hope).

Tuesday the 30th of June
Bivouac 39A. Local carriers disappeared.

When we awoke we discovered what the noises had been from the previous night. The carriers from Ok Bon had disappeared in the night. In the past they had shown little enthusiasm to work as carriers, it was our understanding that they were scared of the mountain. The ghosts of their forefathers lived there and you were supposed to leave them alone. They did not like the fact that we wanted to climb the mountain and predicted great harm for us. The Moejoes, who were from the lower lands, were less troubled by the mountain. They did not know about the evil spirits supposedly on the mountain. They found themselves in a completely unknown territory and didn't understand the language of the locals. This meant they thought it much safer to stay with us.

We spent the whole day exploring the surrounding area of the marsh and the screw pine wood in the neighbourhood. In the evening I was, again, busy drying the samples I had found that day.

Wednesday the 1st and Thursday the 2nd of July
Bivouac 39A. Local Papuans in biak 39A no longer afraid of evil spirits. Not much water available.

During the morning the helicopter flew by in order to inspect the grass area to see whether this would be a suitable landing area. The pilot seemed to think it would be as soon as several more trees were chopped down for safety.

The Papuans from Ok Bon kept coming to our camp more often. They were rather surprised that the evil spirits had still not taken revenge on us because of the climbing going on.

It seemed that our stay in 39A was tolerated by the ghosts which meant that the local Papuans were also no longer afraid to come and visit. They weren't completely content as they were still afraid to go onto the steep ridge above our camp.

It was still good weather, like the last couple of days, we normally had sun in the morning and in the afternoon it often became cloudy but stayed dry. During the rest of the evening the skies would clear up and a cold night would follow. The consistently dry weather meant the pools of water in the marshes kept getting smaller and eventually dried up completely. This made it a lot harder to get our hands on water. In order to still get water a narrow trough had been dug next to the dried up pools, through this enough water seeped for cooking and drinking. There was not enough water to wash. We did not have to worry that we would not have any water at all anymore as there was still a little water running in a very small brook. It was, unfortunately, a lot further from our bivouac than the pools in the marsh.

In the evening we had a good time in our bivouac. Everyone was busy prepping the animals they had found and taking care of the plants. Everything was done by the light of the Tilley lamp and before I went to bed I had to scoop the tree frogs out of my bed again.

Friday the 3rd of July
Bivouac 39A. Supplies by helicopter. Sent post. Van Sprang and Klaarenbeek to 39A by helicopter. Research of treetops. Cut down a screw pine.

After several lower trees had been cut down along the edges of the marsh the helicopter was able to land safely on the grass- if it was nice weather! Several flights took place in order to supply bivouac 39A with supplies from bivouac 39. Van Sprang (radioreporter and filmmaker) and Klaarenbeek (correspondent for *Het Parool*) arrived by helicopter in bivouac 39A from bivouac 39. Van Sprang complained about the fact that he had to pay for all of the flight himself, even this short one from 39 to 39A. He could have saved himself the money as the climb to bivouac 39A was only about an hour, but walking was not his thing so instead he decided to moan and take the helicopter anyway. He didn't like the fact that he had to pay for his food either. You never heard Klaarenbeek complain about anything, the result being that Klaarenbeek fit better into the group, though he did have another problem: falling. He was not used to walking in the jungle which meant that he tripped over tree trunks, and slipped a lot more often than we did as practiced jungle walkers. A couple of our Moejoes quickly noticed this issue and made a railing, though it was rather wobbly and not very reliable. Psychologically it was quite a big help.

Due to the dry weather there was a good chance that the helicopters would start flying again. In preparation, I had written letters home the previous night. With the flight that came in today we also received more letters. For me there was a letter from uncle Wout in which he apologised for his previous letter, which meant we were on friendly terms again. To the letter I had already written to my mother I quickly added some stuff. Because of the rush to make these additions before the helicopter left my handwriting was even worse than it normally was!

As the trees had been cut down so that the helicopter could land I was given the opportunity to inspect the tree tops. It turned out that there were all kinds of mosses growing in the tree tops with a brownish colour from the sun.

Close to our bivouac there were several big screw pines on high set roots. Because I could see a lot of growth in the crowns of these trees and the twigs had big long (about 1 metre) inflorescences hanging from them I decided to cut down these two trees myself. To my surprise this went rather easily, I only had to chop one of the set roots and the tree started to creek and fall down. I had chosen the set roots I chopped carefully so that the tree would not be able to fall on our bivouac. One of the trees had big bunches of fruits and the other was a male with big inflorescences. Cees Kalkman would be able to use these inflorescences for his collection of higher plants. The higher branches were, like the other trees, covered quite thickly with lichens. Here there were thick cuffs of brown mosses and in between these all kinds of very small blooming orchids and ferns. There were also long tendrils of mosses (a lot of *Floribundaria*) hanging from the higher branches. This was a great sample of what was awaiting us in the real moss forest higher up the mountain.

Wim Vervoort, Cees Kalkman, and marine Ferry Brandenburg van den Gronden had now also arrived by helicopter in bivouac 39A.

Saturday the 4th of July
Bivouac 39A. End of the dry spell. Geologists expected back. Communication with the base camp.

On the 4th of July, seven days had passed since the geologist group had left for the top of the Antares. They had taken seven days worth of provisions with them plus some emergency rationing which meant that they could be expected back any minute.

In our bivouac we were able to make a radio connection with Sibil. One of our people had blood in his stool and this meant that we could ask Dr. Romeijn in the base camp what this could be and whether anything could be done about it. Dr. Romeijn then asked, for the whole of New Guinea to hear "Is it hard or soft?". I presume that the problem was not serious as I never heard anything else about it.

It had rained a lot more than we had been used to in the last couple of days. The dried out pool by our bivouac had started to fill itself with water again which was very welcome for the person who fetched the water. At this point we did not know that it would continue raining for days on end.

Sunday the 5th of July
Bivouac 39A. Journey along the drainage creek. Caught a snake. Brongersma visits 39A. Exact location determination by the cadastre group.

It was still good weather and we decided to go for a collecting trip along the drainage stream of the marsh together with the biologist group and Ferry Brandenburg van den Gronden. We followed the stream, along which a path had already been cut for about two kilometres until it merged with a larger stream. The water mingled together and a little later went down like a waterfall along the slope and into the Ok Bon. Where the two streams merged there was a snake warming himself in the sun on a flat stone. Wim Vervoort managed to capture the snake for his collection. The woods along the stream was rather thick and very much shadowed which meant that there weren't very many mosses to be found.

When we arrived back at the camp we were told that Brongersma had visited by helicopter in order to personally form an image of how we lived and worked in the bivouac. The cloud coverage over the Ok Bon Valley had threatened to close up and so he had to leave early, which meant we did not get to meet him.

Fred van der Weiden's job was to determine our exact location as we were close to the border with Australian New Guinea. For this he had brought a bag of cement with him right through the jungle. In order to make his observations he needed a completely stable, horizontal plateau on which he could place his sextant. With the help of one of the marines whom had joined us, the plateau was placed close to our bivouac and cemented under the watchful eye of Fred. The astrophysical observations had to be done on three consecutive nights, so it was now a waiting game for a clear night's sky. Fred had brought an alarm clock with him which went off every hour. When it went off someone needed to check whether the stars could be seen, if they could not they could go back to sleep for another hour until the alarm went off again.

Monday the 6th of July
Bivouac 39A. Composed a rescue team. Van Sprang films the collecting of mosses.

We had still not heard anything from the group of climbers. Thus, it had been decided in the base camp to create a 'rescue team' who would leave from bivouac 39A and climb the mountain in an attempt to find the climbers and help them out if necessary. This team was made up of the marine, Ferry Brandenburg van den Gronden, and several carriers who were led by the marine doctor Tissing who was a good climber. In order to join he had been flown to bivouac 39 and climbed up to bivouac 39A.

In the meantime, Alfred van Sprang had been with me in the marsh in order to film how I looked for, and collected mosses. He had already made similar videos of the others. In his opinion mosses were far too small and could not possibly be important, but for the completeness of the film he still wanted images of me while I was in the field. So the two of us went to the edge of the woods. We also walked past the arum which I had previously seen. Nothing was left of this plant now, only the stem and some leaf fragments. It seemed that Cees Kalkman thought it was big enough to be collected. In the edge of the forest, where I had been many times before, I knew of an area where big colonies of moss grew in abundance and in many different colours. I went to work collecting all of the mosses and putting them in the plastic sandwich bags while I was being filmed. Of course, this was all for show because I had already collected everything I could from this area. After this I showed him the mosses close up and tried to explain to him what research I would later be doing with them. I did not really get the impression that he was interested so we walked back to the camp together.

Tuesday the 7th of July
Bivouac 39A. The rescue team leaves and comes back to bivouac 39A with the geologist group.

The rescue team had left early in the morning along the path which had been created by Escher, Verstappen, and their carriers. After a couple of hours both groups returned back to the bivouac. They had come across each other at about 1700 metres high which was a great relief to everybody.

The climbers who seemed to be undamaged were very wet and exhausted. Everyone wanted to know how the group had managed and how the journey was. They had run into the delay because they had underestimated how long it would take to chop the path. There was also a big rock, at about 2800 metres which blocked the narrow ledge. These delays resulted in them only reaching the West top (3380m.) on the 4th of July, the day they should have arrived back at the camp. At the West top Nicholas stayed behind while Verstappen and Escher went on the next day to highest top. Based on their measurements it appeared that the top was only 3650 metres, rather than the 4000 metres he had previously estimated. After this they went back to the West top, all in the same day, where Nicholas was waiting for them. The next day they started their descent. Verstappen warned us that while we were up there we should not pay too much attention to our compasses, as the rocks towards the top contained a lot of iron.

Of course Van Sprang was also there to record Verstappen's whole story. This was rather difficult because Verstappen kept using certain words and phrases which were not at all suitable to be aired. This caused problems for Van Sprang as it meant that he would have to find a way to cut them out. The fact that Verstappen was doing this on purpose showed how Van Sprang was not very liked among the rest of the group either.

The climbers were given a good meal, which was very welcome as they had spent the last couple of days living off the emergency rations. After having some rest and a big cup of coffee they continued their descent to bivouac 39. From there they would be flown by helicopter to the base camp.

In the evening we had the opportunity to get in touch with the base camp via the radio. The big news was passed on to Brongersma as quickly as possible. Everyone in our bivouac was able to listen in to the radio. The line wasn't very good and this led to some confusion. Somehow Brongersma understood that the climb had not worked, leading to him sighing and saying that this meant the whole expedition had failed. I thought this was rather remarkable. Of course reaching the top was important, but so much had been collected and learnt that the expedition could already be seen as a success. It did not take long before the misunderstanding was rectified and Brongersma understood that the top had indeed been reached. Everyone in bivouac 39A and the base camp was happy that the climb had been a success, and especially that everyone had returned home safely.

Wednesday the 8th of July until Sunday the 12th of July
Bivouac 39A. End of the rainy period. Helicopter lands on the water. Building of bivouac 40.

For the first couple of days in bivouac 39A the weather had been relatively dry but there was a change in the weather around the 5th of July. Every day since then a lot of rain had fallen. In the morning it was sometimes dry for about an hour but by the afternoon the clouds sunk down to the bottom of the valley of the Ok Bon putting us in mist and covering us in rain. This also meant that the stream could no longer take the amount of water and the water level in the marsh kept rising. After several days the rain had changed the initially dry marsh into a lake, in some places it was nearly two metres deep. Luckily our camp was not in danger because we were high above the watershed. Despite the rain and mist I still went out every morning to broaden my collection of mosses. The area was so rich in different kinds that I managed to find new things every day which I could collect and take pictures of. The temperature was rather nice at around 17 degrees in the mist and rain, and if the sun managed to glint through it rose to about 20 degrees. In the evening the temperature dropped to about 14 degrees.

After about five days the weather cleared up and we no longer heard the sound of rain hitting our roof sail. In the morning the sun even shone for several hours. Naturally the helicopters were unable to fly during the rainy period, which also meant that our quickly diminishing food supply could not be replenished.

Now that the sun was shining again and it was also good weather in Sibil it meant that the helicopters could start flying again and our food supply would finally be replenished, and of course, our post would be brought. The helicopters now had to land on water instead of land, which did not cause any issues. When a helicopter had landed it taxied to a provisionally made jetty made from tree trunks next to the ladder to our bivouac. In this way food could be brought to our bivouac without us getting wet feet. The take-off of the helicopter did cause problems however, as when the motor was turned on and the rotors started turning the helicopter started moving round in the opposite direction. This caused some issues and worries that the tail of the helicopter might hit something. The helicopter only stayed still on the water when the tail rotor was turning at full capacity. To stop the helicopter from turning circles someone had to go into the water to hold the helicopter still. Because Wim Vervoort was the strongest and largest person on the trip he offered himself up for this job. Our carriers were not suitable for this work, as as soon as the motor of the helicopter was turned on they got scared and disappeared.

After we knew that climbing the Antares had been successful we could not wait to go and see it for ourselves. For us to be able to do this a semi-permanent bivouac (bivouac 40) was being built at a height of 2360 metres. The marine, Freddy Brandenburg van den Gronden and sergeant de Wijn were sent up with several carriers from the cadastre group to make a clearing for the helicopters and furnish the camp. After several days the bivouac, and the landing area for the helicopters was finished enough for the biologist group to spend the night there. Now we only had to wait for the bivouac to be supplied. Because of the height of the bivouac the amount the helicopters could carry was rather small, so carriers would most likely also be necessary.

Monday the 13th of July
Bivouac 39A. Helicopter makes a reconnaissance flight to bivouac 40. Brongersma in bivouac 39A.

To ensure that the helicopters would actually be able to supply bivouac 40 from bivouac 39 and bivouac 39A Warman made a reconnaissance flight to bivouac 40 in the morning in order to check whether the clearing was suitable for them to land. Upon his return he reported to us that it was fine. However, the helicopters would only be able to land in the morning, as in the afternoon there was almost always too many clouds. Brongersma had joined the helicopter to bivouac 39A to discuss what needed doing further with regards to the research on the Antares. He flew back again by helicopter to Sibil.

Tuesday the 14th of July
Bivouac 39A. Helicopter accident. Van Sprang back to base camp instead of sick Papuan. Evil spirits exist.

In the morning the sun was shining and I headed to the marsh once again to see if I could find something new. The water of the lake had started to descend quite quickly which meant that I could reach the edge of the forest without getting wet feet. I didn't find many new things and as far as I was concerned it was high time we headed to bivouac 40 and the moss forest. It was music to my ears when I heard one of the helicopters flying over to supply bivouac 40. When, after some time we didn't hear the helicopter coming back over we did become slightly concerned. We hadn't heard any loud noises, so we did not think that there had been a crash. Although the sun was still shining where we were we presumed that the clouds must have come in higher up the mountains meaning the helicopter would no longer be able to take off. However, we were still not fully comfortable with the situation. After about two hours of fearful waiting a carrier came running down the mountain out of breath with a note from bivouac 40 saying that the helicopter had crashed. Wim Vervoort came straight to me to tell me the news. To start off with I thought he was making a joke, but Wim is not the kind of person to make jokes about something like this. We were not able to learn anything more from the carrier. This meant we didn't know where the accident had happened or how the pilot was doing. What followed was a big discussion about what we could, and should do, but nobody really had an answer. The only thing we could do was wait for further news. Two hours later, to our great relief, the pilot (Warman), and Mr. Gevelhof from the cadastre group at bivouac 40 arrived in our bivouac unharmed. We were told that during the landing on the clearing of bivouac 40 the helicopter had gotten stuck in a fall wind. Because of this the helicopter dropped too quickly and only landed on the platform with one float, causing the helicopter fall on its side. The rotor blades were crushed in the crash and the whole of the body of the helicopter was severely damaged as well. Warman had gotten stuck with one of his feet, but with the help of some of the carriers he was able to get out of the wreckage safely. Warman was unable to remember this, it appeared that he had been unconscious for a few minutes. When he came to his senses he was stood on the platform looking at what was left of the helicopter. After he had recovered from the shock he and Gevelhof had tripped and slithered themselves down to bivouac 39A in three hours. He thought the helicopter crash was rather traumatic but the descent in the rainforest after this was much worse in his opinion. This was not very surprising as up until this point he had only ever seen the rainforest from the sky. This made the descent an especially gruelling ordeal for him. He told us that he had discovered that jungle walking was not meant for everyone. Because of this one trip he now had great respect for the people who, below him, slowly but surely made their way through the jungle. He spent the night with us and the next day he flew the other helicopter to the base camp.

The radio equipment was no longer worked and we were unable to pass on the news that the helicopter had crashed. Instead of this a runner was sent to bivouac 36 from where messages could be passed on. This journey would take about half a day for someone with practice.

The helicopter crash was big news which had to be sent to Holland as soon as possible. Van Sprang wanted to be the first person to pass this news on. In order to do this, he had to go to the base camp. At this point the only helicopter that was with us was supposed to bring a Papuan carrier back to the base camp who had a jaw infection. This Papuan was already in the helicopter with the motor turning because Warman wanted to take off as soon as possible due to impending clouds in the valley of Ok Bon. Van Sprang was of the opinion that he should be going to the base camp to send his telegram, instead of the sick carrier. So, he pushed the Papuan out of the helicopter and seated himself instead. Warman was so surprised and caught of guard that he still took off to the base camp. The sick Papuan left on foot to the base camp instead, where he arrived three days later. Luckily his jaw infection had not worsened in that time.

The local Papuans were even more convinced now than before the helicopter had crashed that the spirits living in the mountains were very angry because we planned on climbing it and in doing so had disturbed them.

Wednesday the 15th of July
Bivouac 39A. Disagreement with Wim Vervoort.

One of the helicopters was now useless so the supplying and thus the climbing of the Antares by the biologist group was now in danger. Before taking further steps we first waited for instructions from the base camp. There it was decided that the Antares research could be finished, but that, completely understandably, the helicopter was no longer allowed to fly to bivouac 40. This meant that the job of supplying the camp was left completely up to the carriers. We did have several Moejoe carriers with us from the cadastre but these were nowhere near enough to carry all of our belongings for a multiple day trip, the local carriers were now useless because of the evil spirits on the mountain.

As it was uncertain if the biologist group would be climbing the Antares I decided that I would still like to climb up there for one day in order to collect samples from the moss forest. We knew that at about 500 metres above our bivouac this moss forest started because at that height (about 1800 metres) the clouds normally hung making it extra humid. There would probably be a much more lavish collection of mosses with species that could not be found lower down. Wim Vervoort, understandably, did not want us climbing up. Earlier on I had already discussed with Fred whether I (and others if they wanted to join) would be allowed to borrow some of his carriers to go up to the moss forest and return again on the same day. Fred was willing to lend his carriers to me. Several other people also wanted to climb up as they were beginning to get bored in the bivouac and were very curious as to what could be found there and what it would look like. I pitched my idea of making a one day trip the moss forest to Wim Vervoort. I thought it was a very amenable suggestion, especially as it possibly our only option of seeing such an interesting moss forest. I saw no danger, as I was now so experienced with walking through the forests that this would be a relatively easy task. The path had already been cleared and with two or more carriers to join us nothing could go wrong. Wim Vervoort, however, thought it was not a good idea and denied the proposition. I completely disagreed with his decision and really was of the opinion that his attitude was endangering the efficacy of our research in the Antares. At this point, I, completely against my character and, probably too harshly, made my own opinions quite clear to him. A little later Wim Vervoort came up to me to tell me that he could understand my opinion and that I would be allowed to go up the next day. However, he still advised against it and said it was completely my own risk to do so. I was pleased that he had come back on his previous decision, with which, as far as I was concerned, the air was cleared. I do however have the idea that because of my outburst the journey to bivouac 40 was sped up.

Thursday the 16th of July
Bivouac 39A. Reynders and Bril arrive in Bivouac 39A. Preparation for the climb to bivouac 40. Tripod perished.

Now that I had received permission to go to bivouac 40 I wanted to start the climb as soon as possible, as this could be the only chance I got to collect samples from the moss forest. At this point nobody knew for sure whether the biologist group would get the opportunity to go any higher up the Antares. This being said, I left as quickly as possible with three carriers I had borrowed from Fred. The moss forest, also called cloud forest, appeared to start directly above bivouac 39A.

It was going to be a long day and we continued our climb to bivouac 40 in one go without taking breaks. Upon arrival we were heartily welcomed by the people living in bivouac 40. They had heard us coming from a distance and so, had the coffee ready for us. After a long afternoon break we left again back towards bivouac 39A. On our way back we stopped several times to collect mosses. My three carriers also helped me out quite a lot. All of the collected material was put into plastic sandwich bags and after this in a small kit bag. After a long day of collecting and a lot of falling down and getting up again we arrived back in bivouac 39A towards the evening. Here we were welcomed with a warm meal consisting of the usual rice and corned beef. I then heard that Wim Vervoort had decided to go to bivouac 40 with the whole of the biologist group the following day. I was rather pleased to hear this and although this meant that my argument with Wim may not have been necessary it may have sped up the process.

As it was already dark after I had eaten I was not able to dry my newly collected mosses. Above all I no longer had much energy to be able to do this. Instead, I went to bed early in order to get enough rest for the climb the following day.

We were lucky enough that Jaap Reynders, an agro geologist, and corporal Bril where on their way to bivouac 39A from the base camp by way of a longer route along several kampongs. Their goal was to study the soil profile and take samples for later research. Due to the accident with the helicopter his group could no longer be supplied and he had to drastically shorten the journey. After talking the issues through with Brongersma, Reynders decided that he would conjoin his group to the biologist group. This was excellent new for us as Reynders also had a group of 27 Moejoe carriers with him.

Now that we had so many carriers it was possible to properly supply bivouac 40. This made it even more likely that the whole of the biologist group would be able to go up. We spent most of the day readying our personal baggage (collection and drying material, and photo equipment) to be taken to bivouac 40 by carrier. I added a tripod to my things to go up. I had not yet used this tripod very often because it was only suitable for landscape shots and not at all suitable for taking close up pictures of plants. As I did not have much more to do I decided to take some more pictures with the tripod of the marsh. This was not at all a success, as soon as I had readied the tripod in the right position I tripped over one of the legs. This resulted in the leg breaking of completely and the tripod becoming unusable. I decided to leave it in the bivouac instead of bringing it with me. At the end of the day it was probably an awkward thing to bring all the way with me to the top of the mountain anyway.

Friday the 17th of July
Biologist group travels to bivouac 40 with Reynders and corporal Bril. Bril's group goes the wrong way. Play nest of a Bowerbird. The Moss forest.

The most necessary baggage was taken to bivouac 40 by Reynder's carriers, helped by some of the cadastre carriers. The group of carriers, the biologists, Jaap Reynders and corporal Anton Bril climbed up through the moss forest. Before we left we said our goodbyes to Fred van der Weiden and the cadastre people were left on their own in bivouac 39A. They were still waiting for clear skies in order to properly pinpoint the location, but Fred was full of good hope that this would eventually happen.

The first part of the path which had been cut down by the geologists was rather steep. In several places we were forced to climb up on our hands and feet, fortunately, as we got higher it became less steep. There were climbing bamboos hanging everywhere with their nasty thorns and you had to be very careful not to hold on to these. Halfway through the climb we saw the remnants of the bivouac where Escher's group had made camp when they were cutting the path. This is where we also had our break. It was during this break that we noticed that Anton Bril and several carriers were missing. We waited for them for some time before they arrived. It appeared that straight after leaving bivouac 39A they had followed the tributary streams. This path slowly went downhill and they started to doubt whether they were going in the right direction. After about 2 kilometres when the path hit a dead end they returned back to bivouac 39A where they quickly found the right path to bivouac 40. We climbed the rest of the journey together. On our way we also say a play nest of a bowerbird. The nest was made up of a circular shaped wall of moss with, in the middle, some upright twigs and around this a pile of moss with a hole in it. Sadly, we did not see the bird itself.

Most of the carriers did not feel comfortable, as to them this was a completely alien moss forest. You never knew for sure whether the local Papuans were right and there were angry spirits in the woods. This lead to frequent stops in bends of the road so that the Papuans could call out and scare away any possible angry spirits. One of the carriers was allowed to carry the police man's gun, who was with us for protection. The common consensus was that the gun would scare the evil spirits enough that they would not want to hurt us. The carrier felt a lot safer carrying the gun, even though he did not even know how to use or shoot with it.

Upon our arrival at bivouac 40 (2360 metres high) we were welcomed by Ferry Brandenburg van den Gronden, the marine who had organised this bivouac. He had been expecting us and had made up a big pan of pea soup, not an everyday meal for us. This winter food was exactly the right thing after our long and tiring journey in the cold. Most of the carriers were sent back down in order to save on food supplies. On top of this most of the carriers were too afraid to spend the night so high up the mountain because of the evil spirits. We were now able to see the wreckage of the helicopter lying next to the platform. The helicopter seemed so crumpled up it was a miracle the pilot got out of it without being hurt.

Bivouac 40 was a lot more primitive than bivouac 39A because everything had to be brought up by carriers. it consisted of a clearing and two open tents, both made up of a sail on a frame of tree trunks. This meant that the mist and wind had free reign under the sail. One of these tents was used as the kitchen, and the other, bigger one was used for sleeping. There was no separate tent for the carriers. In front of the tents, a Dutch flag had been placed, as it should be.

It was rather cold at this height, especially in the morning when the skies were clearest and so this bivouac was named 'Bivouac Frigidaire'.

We had arrived early in the afternoon so there was more than enough time to do some collecting in the area of the bivouac. The zoologists went in search of insects and birds. In the evening I installed my dry-oven in order to get as much of the collected material as dry as possible.

The Moss Forest

The moss forest usually starts at about 1800 metres, as this is where the clouds often hang. This forest stretches up to about 3000 metres and is a lot more open than the rainforests lower down because the tops of the trees often don't touch. Although there is a lot of mist a lot lighter can enter. This leads to a wide array in the undergrowth of bushes, such as *Rhododendron* and ferns.

The floor, tree stumps, logs and twigs are all covered in a layer of moss, sometimes a metre thick. A small trunk about a centimetre thick sometimes looks like it is a metre thick because of the amount of moss growth. A lot of the floor consists of half rotten tree trunks and toppled stumps, all covered in a thick layer of moss, mostly liverworts. The dead wood and moss makes fixing your footing very difficult and any minute you could find yourself sinking into the undergrowth up to your waist. These holes come into existence when a big tree falls over and the stump rots away. Often the outside of the stump will still look relatively hard but the inside will have rotted away completely creating a big hole often fills with mosses. Often the big colonies of mosses (mostly *Dicranoloma*) and ferns grow on the stumps and twigs. The moss forest is also always very quiet because all noises are dampened immediately by the mossy undergrowth. This creates an almost fairy tale-like atmosphere.

The moss forest on the Antaras has been able to develop itself for the last 5 million years since the mountain was slowly pushed up. It has stood there unchanged since it was created and had never before been seen by white people and probably not by the local inhabitants either because of their fear of the evil spirits which are supposed to live in the woods. After we leave this forest the peace will return and without interruption it will continue to prosper.[7]

It is a place where you are confronted with the eternity. It is only the coming and going of darkness, the drips of water on the leaves and the silent comings and goings of the mist that remind you that time is still going. All days here are the same, there is no change of seasons or weather. The silence is only broken by the infrequent sound of a bird of paradise or the falling of a tree, top heavy from moss and water.

Saterday the 18th of July
Vervoort and Reynders to bivouac 41. Exploring the area around bivouac 40. Drying mosses and collecting insects at the same time.

In the morning a plan was made how to continue the climb of the mountain. As all of our belongings had to be carried up the mountain by carrier our original plan to stay had to be shortened. We only had a few carriers to our disposal who were not too afraid to continue the climb, and so we had to carry parts of our baggage ourselves. We knew that at about 3000 metres high there would most likely not be enough wood to be able to build a bivouac so we had brought a four-person tent with us. Our group however existed of eight people. So it was decided

---

[7] Later we were told that André de Wilde had gone into the moss forest after us even after being explicitly instructed not to by Brongersma.

to divide the group into two. First Wim Vervoort and Jaap Reynders went up with a couple of carriers. They brought the four-person tent with them which would be put up at about 3000 metres high in order to create bivouac 41. The rest of our group would be following them in the following days.

In the last night it had rained a lot but by morning the skies had completely cleared. From the clearing we had an unforgettable view of the area. Dozens of big and small waterfalls had sprung up all over the Antares mass which got smaller and smaller by the hour and then simply disappeared. These were the same waterfalls which we had also heard in bivouac 39A, but that were not visible. Close by you could see the wall and in the shadow the ridge over which we would have to climb further up in order to reach the top of the mountain. From the clearing we could also look into the deep valley of Ok Minam and on the opposite side of the valley we could see, full in the morning sun with the peak in mist, the steep slope going up to the West top of the Antares. We could see from this that we needed to climb up a lot higher if we wanted to get anywhere near to the top. We also had a good view of the area in which somewhere in the distance the Sibil valley must have been situated. In the bright morning sun, we could see, very much in the distance, the mass of the Juliana Mountains which coloured itself from grey to a yellowy red in the light of the sun. This colour spectacle only lasted a few minutes and it didn't take long before all mountains were coloured their natural greyish colour again. We even thought we may be able to see the ice caps of the Juliana mountain. We were so high that we looked down onto the clouds hanging below us in the valleys. After several hours our view was ruined by flecks of mist followed by a thick cover.

In bivouac 39A we had gotten so used to the rain that it no longer stopped us from going out and collecting material in the forest. At that height it was rather cold, but we knew that there would be a warm fire and coffee in the bivouac. In the area, just above the bivouac I was able to collect a lot of samples which I had not seen lower down on the mountain. As usual for a moss forest there were more liverworts than mosses. In the evening I used the dry-oven to dry the collected material as much as possible. We had to be careful with how much petroleum we used for the lamps of the dry-oven as everything now had to be carried up. The zoologists also needed hurricane lights in order to catch insects at night. They would lit up a white piece of sheet hung on some twigs so that the insects would go for the sheet and could easily be caught. We managed to make quite a handy display which meant that the lights from my dry oven also lit up the sheet. In doing this we saved a lot of petroleum, so I tried to dry my mosses as much as possible when it was dark.

Sunday the 19th of July
Going from bivouac 40 to 41 with corporal Bril. Path cut off by a rock. Smoke signals.

In the morning we were awoken early by Anton Bril who was playing a cheerful tune on his harmonica. After a stay of one day in bivouac 40 we had to go further up. I left together with Anton Bril and two carriers who were carrying a small sail, early n the morning. After less than 500 metres of walking through the moss forest we came upon a big rock in the middle of our path of about 2900 metres high which was exactly on the ridge we needed to climb over in order to get to the top. On both sides of the rock there was an extremely steep slope, on the right to the 1500 metre deeper Ok Bon river and on the left to the even deeper Ok Bon. The rock was covered in several trees and bushes and there were roots from these all over the rock. To get past it we had to shuffle ourselves step by step over the roots and hold on to them without hands. We also had to make sure we didn't look down into the depths so that we didn't get dizzy. With our face practically pressed up against the rock we crawled over the distance of about 30 metres, slowly across. The Reynders group had already passed this area the day before and they had made a kind of banister of rattan which made us feel a little safer. Our whole group made it over the rock without falling. I did see a lot of small plants with nice white flowers on the rock, maybe *lobelia*, and a lot of mosses. But because I needed both my hands to avoid falling I was unable to collect anything.

Shortly after this, at about 3000 metres, the woods changed in character. The trees became lower and the bushes and undergrowth increased making it harder to find the path which had been created by the geologists. The line between the two kind of forest was not a direct one and here and there parts of moss forest could still be found. In some places the bushes grew very close on each other, making it a difficult for us to pass. In some places we had to walk over the lower bushes in order to make progress.

Here, about at the border of the moss forest and the shrub vegetation, at about 3000 metres high we found the tent that had been put there by the Reynders group as Bivouac 41. One of the carriers had stayed with the tent while Jaap Reynders and Wim Vervoort had climbed on to the West top. They returned back at the tent at about the same time as we did. The climb up and down to the West top had been rather tiring, upon return Wim laid down and sighed that he would be doing nothing else that day. At the top it had been very good. They had even found a pool of water there which was very important because there was hardly any water on the ridge. We had had to bring water from the previous bivouac for our coffee and some water could be collected my squeezing out the moss but this was it. For the two carriers the sail was set up. This bivouac only existed of a double roofed tent and a small tent sail. This all for six people.

The area where the tent was on was slightly sloped as there was no level area to be found. After everything had been properly installed I had some time to explore the area and collect as much as possible.

We were sat just above the moss forest in a subalpine shrub vegetation. But in between the bushes there were still parts of the moss forest, although the trees were less tall. A particularly noticeable tree was a kind of pine tree (*Papuacedrus papuana*) of which the branches grew horizontally at the base and then protruded upwards with a curve, because of the shape this created we called these the candlestick trees. Another interesting plant was a bush with bright red stamen flowers (*Mearnsia*) and an orchid (*Dendrobium*) mostly with red but sometimes also white flowers which were scattered along the path we were walking at this height.

We had agreed with the people at bivouac 40 that, if the weather permitted, we would send out smoke signals so that they would be able to see where we were situated on the mountain. The weather had been quite good with sun and mist and towards the evening the skies cleared completely. We were also in rather open terrain so that it was ideal to send off smoke signals. The fire that was already going for our coffee water was stoked by our carriers and damp plant matter was laid on the fire so that it started smoking.

Although our tent was meant for four people I still thought the space was too little and preferred to sleep on the floor under the sail with the two Papuans that were still with us. In the warmth of a blanket under a sail I could see the surroundings. The candlestick trees were clearly visible as dark silhouettes in the moonlight. Every now and then a patch of mist would come by under the sail, only to clear up to the moon shining again. During the whole night you could hear the sound of the frogs in the area, enhancing the fairy tale atmosphere. It had been a good choice to sleep under the sail, as if I had slept in the tent I would have missed out on this experience.

Monday the 20th of July
From bivouac 41 to 42. Mouth harmonica concert. Brongersma by runner. Cooking rice in the lid of a carrying tin.

In the early morning, towards sunrise, we were awoken by a cheerful mouth harmonica concert by Anton Bril. The popular Dutch song 'Wake up the sun is already up' was played as usual but also a lot of other popular songs. With a concert like that our day had a cheerful start, and our carriers thought it was great as well. On top of this we had a great view of the area. This time we were sure that we could see the ice top of the Juliana top. Anton Bril and the carriers were mastered in the art of making fire so they were able to treat us to warm rice and coffee in the early morning.

The idea was that we would move the bivouac to the area of the West top (bivouac 42) with the four of us where Reynders and Vervoort had already been. We only had two carriers with us, and with the tent to carry now, we allhad to help carrying. Anton Bril offered to carry as much as possible on his back so he ended up having the heaviest load. Still, we were unable to carry everything and we had to leave the fly sheet of the tent behind. The two carriers would walk back to bivouac 41 later on and take the rest of the baggage to bivouac 42.

Just above bivouac 41 the 1 to 2, sometimes 5-metre-high bushes started to appear. In the damper areas there were more and more sub-alpine meadow with lots of mosses (especially *Dicranoloma*) and several alpine flowers (*Gentian* and *Euphrasia*) that looked a lot like the alpine flowers which grow in the European alpine meadows. Just as I was taking pictures of the gentians a Papua came running up to us out of breath with a letter from Brongersma that had come in at bivouac 36 radiographically. The message was that we had to keep our stay at the top of the Antares limited to one day because of the limited supply of food. This had been our plan anyway so there was no need for us to make any changes. Jaap Reynders, who was sat next to me by the gentians, was extremely concerned by Brongersma's note because he has misunderstood it in all the excitement. He had read that Brongersma wanted us to return back immediately and not finish our journey to the top. In his excitement he left his lighter by the gentians which did not do the photo any good, this is the only picture with a lighter in it! We told him to read the note again, properly this time. When he did this he quickly calmed down. Eventually he also found his panic rather funny and was able to laugh off the whole affair.

The steep slope that we were climbing up was only covered with a thin layer of peaty soil which was held together by the roots of the grassy vegetation and several bushes. The ground was soaked from the rain, and because of the closeness of the rock it was hard for the excess water to disperse. The result of this was that sometimes when we put a step up we would slide down again, also because of the weight on our back. This meant that we had to continue on all fours which meant that we were able to climb more quickly until it no longer worked. Luckily there were more bushes here and we were able to hold on to these to stop us from slipping down.

At about 3200 metres the ground was dryer and the vegetation was like European heaths because of the metre-high bushes. It was remarkable that in this area there were still areas of woods of which the trunks and branches on the trees were heavily laden with mosses (a lot of *Macromitrium*). The moss was mostly coloured brown, like it had been at bivouac 39A and 41, due to the great amount of sunlight.

At a depression along the mountain ridge at about 3300 metres close to the West top (3380 metres) we found an area that was relatively flat. This is where we decided to set up bivouac 42 (existing of the same tent as bivouac 41). As we had not brought the fly sheet of the tent with us to save weight we attached plastic bags to both tent poles to avoid rain coming in. Not long after this Anton Bril and Jaap Reynders made a fire and we could enjoy warm coffee again.

The two carriers were so exhausted and numb from the extra cargo and the cold that we could not possibly make them go up and down again for the rest of the baggage left behind in bivouac 41. Instead we sent them back down to bivouac 41 and they did not have to come back up again. This meant we were at the West top without a fly sheet for the tent and apparently also without my blanket which had been forgotten- it was going to be a cold night! One of our carriers had also accidentally left behind a pan on during the break, which meant Anton Bril had to improvise when it came to making our dinner. He managed to use a lid from a carrying tin as a pan to cook the rice. Naturally the rice did not cook properly at this height, but everything tastes good if you are hungry enough.

It was still early in the afternoon and the weather was quite good, so I investigated the area and collected some samples. The diversity of kinds was a lot less than it was lower down, but the species were mostly different. As I had been unable to bring my dry-oven with me I put all of the collected materials into plastic sandwich bags. As long as this was not exposed to direct sunlight, the material would keep for a couple of days.

When we woke up in the morning we were not woken with Anton Bril's tunes, but instead by the rain hitting our tent. Within the tent we were not completely dry as the rain came through the sail like a fine mist.

Here we were, just under the equator, in a tent with the four of us without a fly sheet, in a thick fog and streaming rain, with the temperature just above zero on a mountain top that no one had ever been on before. This last part was not completely true as the geologists Herman Verstappen, Arthur Escher and lieutenant Nicolas had cut this road leading to the top a week before. The only thing we could do while it kept raining was stay in the tent. A positive note to this weather was that the clouds had stopped the temperature from getting as cold as we were worried about, especially because we only had three blankets between the four of us. We couldn't permit ourselves to get wet at these low temperatures because we didn't have any dry clothes.

Around eleven o'clock it stopped raining and the mist disappeared so we could get up. Only Wim Vervoort stayed in the tent because he felt ill. After enjoying the scenery for some time we saw the mist rise from the valley of the Ok Bon and sure enough we were soon enveloped in it. Every now and then the mist would dissipate and the West top would become visible. We were also able to see the highest top (East top 3650 metres) through the mist but it quickly disappeared behind the mist for the rest of the day. Luckily the weather stayed dry which meant we were able to collect and photograph a lot here as well as on the West top.

There had been thundering and roaring noises all through the night which we hadn't heard before. We were able to see what the cause of this was when the mist intermittently rose. Waterfalls had come into existence varying from several decimetres to several metres. After several hours the sound seemed to disappear, as did the waterfalls themselves.

We tried to walk to the highest top but it didn't take long before we decided this would probably be irresponsible because of the clouds rising from the valley of the Ok Bon. We also came to the realisation that it would be a lot better to head to the West top instead of the East top as it would take a lot less time. This would mean that we would have more time to collect material and take photos. Originally we had expected to spend a day longer but we had to make space for the next group, so we had to be as efficient as possible with the little time we had.

At the start of the afternoon we went to the West top. Wim Vervoort had also risen out of bed. He felt better and thought he would be able to join us for the last part of the climb. The West top was only 80 metres above our tent at a height of 3380 metres and about a kilometres walk. The path leading to it had heath-like vegetation with a lot of Ericaceae (*Vaccinium, Rhodondendron* etc.), ferns, grasses and mosses. An interesting find was the moss *Rhacocarpus purpurascens*.[8] Surprisingly there were still several trees at this height which were thickly covered by mosses and scattered with orchids. Close to our tent there was a small square pool which Wim Vervoort had already told us about and where we could get our water from. At the bottom of this pool there was a big *Breutelia*.[9] At the West top there was also a striking *Rhodondendron* with rather large white flowers which I photographed. Later it turned out that this plant was a new kind to science, as a specialist (Dr. Sleumer from the herbarium in Leiden) could see from the image. I was focusing on the collection of lower plants and did not collect any samples of this *Rhododendron*. This would not have worked anyway as I did not have any newspapers to dry the samples in, meaning that to my knowledge my picture is the only record of this *Rhodondendron*, and the variety has still not been described.

As we (other than the geologists) were the first people to ever climb the West top of the mountain we wanted to leave behind a sign that we had been there. At the top we buried a plastic bottle with two notes. The first note was an official paper with the emblem of the marines and Anton Bril's name on it. On the other note we wrote our own names: Jaap Reynders, Wim Vervoort and Ben van Zanten. After this we discussed whether this bottle would ever be dug up, or whether erosion would wash it away into the valley of the Ok Bon and from there via the Ok Tsjop and the Digoel and end up in the sea and wash up somewhere.

Everything taken into account, even the rain from the morning, I was rather satisfied with the mosses and lichens I had collected. I did think

---

8   Finding this kind of moss on the West top was the main reason for my research into the possibility of long distance spreading of mosses as I later find the same kind in New Zealand.

9   This kind was later described by me as *Breutelia aristifolia* Zanten and was new for science.

it a shame that I was unable to collect the mosses growing on the acidic crystalline rocks at the highest top, that Herman Verstappen had told us about. Without a doubt species would be found there that I had now missed out on.

Wednesday the 22nd of July
'Flying saucer'. Icecap on the Juliana top. In the mist. Back to bivouac 40.

This morning we were awoken by the sound of 'The sun is already up' again and the sun was indeed shining, with clear skies and no rain the previous night. We were glad that it was time to get up as it had been very cold. The view was once again phenomenal; in the distance we could see the view of the Juliana mountain peak with its icecap shining in the sun. Jaap Reynders and I were, during our morning toilet, enjoying the view when Jaap tapped me and said: 'Look at that, what is it?'. In the distance against the dark background of the Juliana mass we could see a small speck of light which was slowly moving completely horizontally from the north to the south. We could follow the speck of light until it became invisible against the lighter background of the sky. At this time there was a lot of talk about flying saucers and we decided we had seen one too. Of course neither of us really believed this, but we didn't know how else to explain it. Later we did ask whether there had been any planes in the area at that time and place but we were told that this was not the case. Eventually Jaap and I decided that it must have been a reflection from the sun on the interface of two different air levels. Whether this was true or not we do not know but it meant we had a possible explanation.

With our two carriers, who had spent the night in bivouac 41, we had previously agreed that they would return to bivouac 42 (our tent) to carry our baggage back to bivouac 40. They must have gotten up and left early because they showed up around 9 o'clock. All of our baggage was readied for transporting. It was mostly made up of our sleeping stuff and the collected material. The tent was staying up for the next group. We had placed a flag on a long stick by the tent so that it would be easier for the next group to find. Wim Vervoort and Jaap Reynders would head off first and Anton Bril and I, together with the carriers would head down last. I wanted to look at some more mosses just under the bivouac because I had not collected anything there yet. It was dry weather with a good view, but I was only just started on my way before a fog bank came up from the valley. Before I even realised I was completely surrounded by fog and I could not see more than ten metres in front of my face. I had strayed a little from the path whilst collecting and became completely disorientated. Luckily I had followed Dr. Van der Sleen's advice and had marked my path by breaking off twigs so that I could backtrack my steps. Shortly after this the fog cleared and I was able to see the West top again, and after about ten minutes I managed to find the path. Due to the shock I hadn't actually collected anything. In the distance I could hear Anton Bril and the two Papuans coming. The four of us then continued on down the mountain. In the place were bivouac 41 had been we passed the second group on their way to bivouac 42 (the tent). They had left bivouac 40 very early so that they could get straight to bivouac 42 as there was no tent at bivouac 41 anymore. After we had exchanged all of our adventures both groups went in their own direction. It was not long before we got back to the moss forest and passed the big rock. About half way through the afternoon we arrived back in bivouac 40.

Of course we were met with coffee by the people of the cadastre that were present in the bivouac. I still had enough time to install the dry-oven and dry a large part of the collected material.

Thursday the 23rd and Friday the 24th of July
Bivouac 40.

I spent these two days drying my collected materials. When the oven was filled it always took several hours before the mosses were dried. During the drying process the material had to be turned over in order to also dry the top of the mosses. There was still a lot of opportunities to collect some more stuff. Luckily it didn't become really foggy which meant I could still collect, and a Papuan from the cadastre now always joined me who I already knew from the trek from Woropko to the base camp.

Saturday the 25th July
From bivouac 40 to 39. Van der Weiden still waiting for clear skies. Carrier with wound on his foot.

The descent from the moss forest to bivouac 39A went quickly and we rested again at what was left of the temporary bivouac built by Escher. A large portion of our food supplies had been used and one of the aluminium carrying tins was empty. This we left behind. The tin will probably remain there for centuries until it is completely perished. On our way up to the top we had thought the moss forest very interesting but we were now so used to it that it was nothing special anymore.

Upon arrival at bivouac 39A we had the feeling that we were arriving home after being gone for a long time. Everything was unchanged, even Fred van der Weiden was still sat on the same bench waiting for the three consecutive starry nights necessary for the triangulation. He had still been unable to make his observations but this had had no effect on his mood. He was still cheerful and full of good hope that he would eventually get lucky. At this point he was not aware that he would have to wait until the beginning of September.

We only stayed in bivouac 39A for a short period and went straight on to bivouac 39 at the shore of the Ok Bon. Just before we were about to leave one of the Moejoe carriers who was going to join us to the base camp came to me and showed me his foot. It seemed that he had stood on something sharp which had created a scratch that had become a sore. I cleaned the wound well and disinfected it with iodine and stuck a big plaster and a bandage on it. Luckily the wound was on the cavity of his foot so that he was able to walk carefully. We did make sure that for the rest of the journey to Sibil he did not have to carry anything.

Sunday the 26th of July

From bivouac 39 to 36. Local carriers enthusiastic to join. André de Wilde unexpectedly in bivouac 36.

All of our baggage had to go back to the base camp. The only helicopter we had left was unable to take all of us and our baggage and so Brongersma had asked us to walk back. I was quite pleased about this because, in the helicopter you only see the river and mountains from above and it was like watching a movie. Walking was a lot more interesting as you really experienced the journey. Walking also meant that we would be able to meet the friendly inhabitants that we hadn't see by our bivouac.

For the journey we needed the Moejoe carriers and several more locals. To our surprise it was not too hard to get a couple of men to come with us. Going down the mountain would not anger any evil spirits. The fact we had not come across any problems on the climb up the mountain was also taken to mean that the spirits were fine with our presence there. The locals were also quite interested in seeing the base camp, most of them had never been before and saw it as an exciting adventure. Early in the morning, when we were still eating rice and drinking coffee the aspiring carriers came to us from the surrounding kampongs. Big and small everyone wanted to come along. A couple of small boys, who seemed to have overslept came running up at the last minute to join us. Sadly, not everyone could join. The idea was that we would go to bivouac 36 first and stay there for a couple of days.

After everyone had made their own baggage convenient to easily carry, the convoy was ready to leave. The path followed the OK Bon as bivouac 36 was close to its banks. The slopes had several kampongs on them which meant our route went partly over the local roads and secondary forest. On the first part, the cut path went under the bushes of the spiny climbing bamboo which meant we had to go through this part bent double, making it extra tiring. We were passing the kampongs and gardens which I had seen from the helicopter on my way to bivouac 39. The gardens were, as in the Sibil valley, surrounded by a kind of fencing made from plaited twigs to protect them from wild pigs. The plants that I saw were primarily sweet potatoes, sugar cane, keladi and a lot of weeds.

On the route we also had to cross a side river of the Ok Bon four times. Our path went quite high along the slope of the Ok Bon making the side rivers rather deep. The large amount of rain from the last days caused the rivers to be heavy with water, but this did not cause much trouble for us. In several areas the steep slopes down to the brooks and then the steep slopes up again caused us extra difficulty. Everything was very slippery and I fell in the mud several times. Eventually we all arrived at bivouac 36 very wet and dirty.

The bivouac was rather high (1200 metres) up the slope of the last, big side river (Ok Tenman) of the Ok Bon and we had a beautiful view of the Antares mass that we had just come from. After our evening meal we did not do anything else. We were going to spend several days here so we would have more than enough time to explore the area and collect mosses in the coming days.

During our journey I once again gained great appreciation for our Papuans. They hardly ever fell over and they laughed a lot on the way, even though they had almost 20 kilos on their back on the steep and slippery paths. Naturally the smaller boys received a smaller load to carry.

When we were sat around talking about the journey we heard the helicopter arriving and to our surprise André de Wilde got out. He was busy with an anthropological investigation in the neighbourhood of the Antares. He had also heard about the moss forest on the mountain and wanted to see this with his own eyes. For his research it was not necessary to go there as not a single Papuan dared to go into the forest because of the evil spirits. This meant Brongersma did not give him permission to go. But, stubborn as he was, he had asked the helicopter pilot to fly him to bivouac 36 himself. From what he told us, his plan was to go to the moss forest on the Antares. We knew that he hadn't gotten permission for this trip and because of this he received a rather cool welcome when he arrived. Of course he noticed this, and his reply to this was: 'It seems like I'm not very welcome here.' This was the case, but he was allowed to spend the night at bivouac 36, after this it was up to him to find his way to the moss forest.

Monday the 27th of July until Friday the 31st of July
Bivouac 36. Kampong Nimdol. Cassowary. Tobacco. Harness. Powellia. Second group of biologists back from Antares.

Bivouac 36 was relatively luxurious and was well supplied by our helicopters so there was more than enough food. Kampong Nimdol was close by. This was a neat kampong which looked just like the kampongs close to our base camp. There was not much to see in the houses, only a fireplace and for as far as I could see the roofs did not leak. It was striking that the inside of the fence had been planted full of keladi. As usual the villagers were friendly and helpful, and eager to show us all kinds of things. Close to the houses a cage had been made where they kept a cassowary. We knew these birds were native to the area because we often saw the feathers used as decoration during the dance parties, but we had not seen a live one before.

In and around the kampong people had planted tobacco. In order to dry the tobacco a network of twigs had been built which faced the sun. The tobacco leaves were tied together in small bundles and put on this network to dry.

One of the boys from the kampong, who was a little misshapen, showed us a harness he had built in case there were fights with neighbouring kampongs. He demonstrated how you were supposed to wear it, but got into trouble because his penis shaft got in the way. You could see him pondering about what to do. He could not take the shaft off as this was considered embarrassing. Eventually he figured it out and turned his back to us to sort everything out before turning back. Funnily enough the harness only covered and protected the top half of his body.

The couple of days that we spent here I spent exploring the area. I mostly collected from the valley and from the low slopes of the Ok Tennam. This gave me a great variety of sorts of mosses, although the slopes were rather overgrown and full of climbing bamboo. The most interesting find was a *Powellia*,[10] I could see that this was a new species for science

---

[10] This new species was described by me as *Powellia subelimbata* Zanten spec. nov.

as I had previously been working on a revision of this group. This species grew on periodically flooded stones in the Ok Tennam.

When I was collecting in the valley I was often visited by a friendly man with a big pig's tooth in his nose with a button on top. He seemed to be curious as to what I was doing and offered to carry the plastic bags of collected material for me. Sometimes a couple of women came and watched me, though I never saw any children.

Towards the end of the afternoon on the 31st of July the second group of biologists arrived (Cees van Heijningen, Cees Kalkman, and John Staats, and Brandenburg van den Gronden) with a group of carriers from the Antares. They had also experienced rain and mist cover the top, stopping them from reaching it. Herman Verstappen and Arthur Escher (both geologists) would then remain the only people to ever have reached the highest top of the Antares. If we had stayed on the Antares a day longer as we had originally planned we would not have reached the top either, and so it seemed that our shortened stay did not mean much difference. It had still been hard for the second group to find our tent, even with the stick and flag we had placed by it.

Saturday the 1st of August
From bivouac 36 to bivouac 34A. Young man with hair knot. Two men with one blanket.

After we had breakfast together we made our baggage ready together with the carriers in order to leave for bivouac 34A on the Ok Tsjop. Several of the carriers from the Ok Bon, who had taken our things from bivouac 39 to bivouac 36, had gone home. It seemed that they had decided that it was either too far or too long a journey to go all the way to the base camp. This meant that we needed some more carriers from the Nimdol to carry our equipment to the base camp. This was not a problem as there were enough men who wanted to join. After this had all been arranged we left together for bivouac 34A.

The area that we were trekking through (the Kiwirok) was rather hilly and there were several stream in the valleys that we had to cross. In comparison to the slopes along the Ok Bon, which were rather dense, this area was more sparsely vegetated. The route went partly through the local paths in the rainforest but also through paths which had only recently been created by the geologists. We only came past an abandoned garden once. During our break I was able to collect more mosses. Halfway through the afternoon we arrived in bivouac 34A where we saw the rattan bridge which went over the Ok Tsjop (East-Digoel) and right behind it a 500-metre-high wall, which was very steep. I reckoned that this was the abyss that Sneep and Herberts had seen from above, making them the first white people to see it. The next day we would have to climb this wall in order to get over the watershed between the Ok Tsjop and the Ok Sibil.

The bivouac was situated on the north shore of the Ok Tsjop just above the river. It existed only of awning which had been stretched out over poles. I did not see any kampongs in the neighbourhood but they probably were there, considering the number of Papuans who joined us. One of these Papuans was a young man who wore a red knot of hair on the back of his head like we had seen people sporting in the base camp.

Although the bivouac was only 800 metres high it had been quite cold the previous night and a blanket really was necessary. For unknown reasons my blanket had not been brought which meant I had to share with my sleeping buddy. This went just fine until one of us turned around and pulled the blanket off of the other person, in turn meaning the blanket had to be pulled back. This happened several times during the night but we were still relatively rested the next morning.

Sunday the 2nd of August
From bivouac 34A to the base camp. Hanging bridge. Tenmasigin.

For the last part of our journey back to the base camp we had to go over the watershed between the valley of the Ok Tsjop and the Ok Sibil. We started with a short descent to the rattan bridge over the river we had already seen from above. The bridge was in a rather good state because another group had crossed it and repaired it just before us. This saved us a lot of time, although the crossing of a bridge still takes a long time if you are with a big group of people. The bridge was about 50 metres long and you could never have more than one person crossing it at a time. During the walking, or rather shuffling, over the thin strands of rattan we had to hold on tight to the railings with both hands. You also had to make sure never to look down. If you did look down it would appear as if the water was stood still and the bridge was moving with great speed. I knew this very well, as did our Moejoe carriers, as we had gone over similar bridges in the neighbourhood of Katem. Though the bridge creaked a lot everyone crossed without any troubles.

When everyone had crossed the bridge the long and very steep climb started out of the Ok Tsjop valley. We had to conquer a height difference of about 500 metres. On the other side there was some sign of where the path began. As usual the path was slippery and covered in tree trunks so a great deal had to be done on all fours. Slipping and falling over was something which was done frequently by us, but not by our carriers. Eventually we all managed to get to the top safely and from there the path became easier. It went through hilly terrain of rainforest and bits of secondary forest and slowly rose more. It seemed that there used to be gardens here. The whole area was sparsely populated and we didn't come across any kampongs.

The watershed was at about 1600 metres and not far from the Tenmasigin area, from where Wim Vervoort with the Reynders group had collected mosses for me during my absence at the Sibil. After we reached the watershed the path started to descend slowly to the Sibil valley at about 1200 metres. This was a relatively easy part though it was still rather hilly and full of tree trunks. Slowly the terrain started to become more familiar as I had been there before with my two friends from the base camp.

Once we arrived in the base camp we were greeted cheerfully by those who were present. Here, I met Neijenhuis (blood group specialist) for the first time who had come from Tanah Merah to our base camp while we were on the Antares. He had been in the Sibil before but had not been able to do anything because he did not have his equipment. He had taken the helicopter to Tanah Merah to look for his equipment, and he was very proud to tell me that he had found all of his equipment in Tanah Merah and had walked back to the Sibil with it through the same route that I had previously taken.

A good meal was made for us all and we were able to rest from the long journey we had had. Firstly, we read the mail which was waiting for us at the camp. Among the mail was a tape with a sound recording which we could not listen to because we did not have the right equipment. There were also letters from Jan, Uncle Wout, Hilly, mother and so on. After I had read my mail I washed my clothes and myself in the Sibil, as we had hardly had the chance to do anything like that in the past couple of days. I also wrote several letters back home about my most recent adventures as it was likely that a plane would come the next day. I was rather pleased to be able to sleep in my trusted bed of jute bags, a blanket and a mosquito net.

Although we had not managed to reach the highest top of the Antares I was very satisfied with the results of our endeavour. I was also happy about not having to take the helicopter back to the Sibil. The three days it took to get through the rainforest was not only more interesting but had also provided me with some interesting samples.

Monday the 3rd of August until Thursday the 6th of August
Basecamp. Tree-kangaroos. Chicken-pox. Cineast Ter Laag arrives to film the journey to the Juliana Mountains. Cookies from Van Sprang.

One of the most interesting animals that the Papuans brought back to bivouac 39 was a living tree-kangaroo, a marsupial which lives in trees and is about half a metre tall with a long tail and relatively short legs with which he walked and did not jump as kangaroos do. The animal was flown to the Sibil by helicopter where a nice cage was made for him. The idea was to gift the animal to Diergaarde Blijdorp in Rotterdam.

A couple of our carriers had become sick in the Antares bivouac 39A. They had contracted chicken-pox and had come back to the base camp without baggage, where they arrived after three days. This was quite a feat for the sick carriers. Based on advice given by Dr. Romeijn a small bivouac was built for them behind the cadastres bivouac. Luckily the disease did not spread any further.

During an earlier supply drop for all of the expedition members, Van Sprang had received a Verkade-tin filled with all kinds of cookies. We had found out that Van Sprang did not like all the biscuits and only ate the luxurious cookies. Because of his annoying attitude on the Antares someone made up a plan to tease him a little. One afternoon when he was not around, we exchanged all of the cookies he liked for the biscuits he did not. He must have discovered that this happened, but he never said anything about it.

The filmmaker Ter Laag arrived on Wednesday the 5th of August in order to film the journey to the Juliana Mountains.

Friday the 7th of August
To Oemboek with the giant bananas.

Halfway to the kampong Kigonmedib lay a doline that was called 'Oemboek' in the Sibil language. This means 'valley of the giant bananas'. I had heard from Kalkman, Anceaux, and De Wilde, who had already been, that there was indeed a group of giant bananas and that there were also small caves in the limestone. Oemboek was the only place where these giant bananas grew. It seemed that there was a special environment there, which meant that there may well be different kinds of mosses there as well. I wanted to see this place, so I organised to go there with my two friends and some other boys who brought hurricane lamps with them to see into the caves. One of our marines also joined us and an older Papuan as a guide. I did not need to organise the guide; the boys did this themselves.

We left in the morning and started the journey by wading through the Sibil. After about a half an hour walk along the path towards Kigonmedib we reached the Oemboek. The lavish vegetation of the surrounding rainforest meant that the sinkhole was not immediately noticeable, but suddenly we were looking into a pit of about 40 metres deep, with a diameter of 150 metres. The pit had the typical funnel shape of a doline with very steep sides. Through the other vegetation we were looking down at the tops of several giant banana trees that were stood on a steep slope of the 'Valley of the Giant Bananas' in a group. The term 'valley' is not really appropriate here because this implies more of a river valley which was definitely not the case. There was no water in this doline, as there was in the doline close behind our camp. We then went along the steep slope, which largely consisted of wet clay and and rocks and slipped ourselves down. Several times, when I stood on a rock or clay block I nearly fell down, but when this happened I was immediately caught by one of the boys. This meant that I did not fall properly once. Here and there on the slopes it could be seen that, with heavy rainfall, small streams were formed leading towards the bottom of the doline where the water appeared to disappear in the ground.

There was a lot of hedged mosses and especially giant ferns that were like carpets hanging down the walls. There were quite a few mosses growing on the rocks and bushes, I didn't collect these because they were strongly etiolated due to the lack of light and I couldn't reach them properly. A lot of the mosses were also partly covered in mould. In places where it was more open we saw big spiders who were sat very still in their web, but if you touched the web or the spider they started shaking strongly to try and scare us off. The big spiders were the females and the tiny males were sat on the females. I had seen this kind of spider before at the base camp.

The depth and the heavy growth of the doline made it seem as if it was twilight and there was only a little sun here and there. In an area that was slightly less steep the giant bananas were stood in a group of about 20. I estimated that the height of the biggest giant banana was about 10 to 15 metres and they had a diameter of 70 to 80 centimetres, too large to put your arm around the trees. On some of the trees there were bunches of relatively small bananas. At the foot of the big trees there were smaller trees ready to take over. The bananas were, like most wild bananas, not edible and were full of shiny black pips, as I had already heard from my friends.

We crawled out of the doline on the other side, which was less steep and slippery than the side we entered. The biggest part of the slope consisted of sharply formed limestone. At a certain point, still deep in the doline, there was a big overhanging rock from which slowly but constantly water was trickling down from the rocks above. This meant that the rocks underneath were constantly wet and thus were covered in a slimy type of green algae. Sadly, I did not find any mosses here, I presume because it was too dark. We also saw a small opening, just large enough for an adult, that led into a small cave. I thought it was too scary to go enter but our marine was willing to go and of course so did the Papuan boys. They looked around the cave with a hurricane lamp. They did not find anything, even the bats that had been spotted previously were not there.

Close above this cave there was another small opening to a cave. According to the Papuans this was taboo and nobody dared go in as ghosts were supposed to live there. I presume that the highest cave was the real cave of 'Oem'. As we climbed higher-up the slope there were several places where the sunlight could reach and there were some interesting plants growing on the limestone, like a cuckoo-flower and probably a *Lobelia* that was a lot like the one on the big rock above bivouac 40 on the Antares. After this we climbed, here and there on all fours, out of the doline and went back to the base camp feeling fulfilled.

Saturday the 8th of August
Base camp. Group Bär leaves for the trek to Hollandia. Mail bag comes with. De Wilde crippled back from Antares. Van der Weiden last one in bivouac 39A.

This morning the group Bär, after saying their lengthy goodbyes, left for the trek to Hollandia. Saying goodbye was actually done twice, the first time was a fake goodbye and was filmed by Ter Laag, Klaarenbeek, Van Sprang and others. The second time was the real goodbye which was not filmed.

A small mail bag also went with the group with letters from the expedition members. Jan Sneep, our 'post master' in the Sibil stamped the letters (with expedition stamp) and an extra stamp was added with the text 'Doorsteek Sibil Hollandia' (Trek Sibil Hollandia) and with the signatures of Bär and Dasselaar. On their way another stamp would be added from the 'post office' in Waris, along the route to Hollandia, in the middle of the jungle. These letters will without a doubt become something special for the collectors.

Not long after the Bär group left, the group of carriers left with the marine doctor Tissing towards the kampong Denmatta on route to the Juliana top. Just after this André de Wilde came walking back to the base camp from the Antares. He had had a heavy journey because his ankle had started playing up and he could not walk properly. He told us that in the past he had been operated on the ankle due to an accident with a moped. They had then placed a pin in his ankle that was still there. He also told us that after his stay with us in bivouac 36 he went to the moss forest. Naturally he couldn't do anything for his own research there because no people lived there, but we knew that already. André was the last researcher who was in the moss forest of the Antares. His leave meant that the nature could continue its work and the angry spirits could let their anger go. Bivouac 39A could be dismantled except for a place for the cadastre group, because Fred van der Weiden was still waiting for a succession of clear nights.

Sunday the 9th of August
Plan for biologists to Juliana Mountains. Talk with Brongersma.

Brongersma asked me if I still wanted to join the geologist group to the Juliana Mountains and how many carriers I would need for that. He told me that he wanted to try and get the geologists, and the biologists to Denmatta and further on to the Juliana Mountains. I told him that I would very much like to go and estimated that I would need about three carriers for the journey. Wim Vervoort and John Staats did not see the point of joining as there would not be any mammals or birds up that high. Cees Kalkman and Cees van Heijningen were eager to go but they would need more carriers for their research. Brongersma could not guarantee anything because the supply of food and especially petrol for the helicopter was very unsure.

He told us that he had great respect for the geologists, biologists and the people from the cadastre who tirelessly made their way through the rainforest to collect their research material. Brongersma also made the remark that there were some people in the camp who had 'rainforest fear'. He did not name any names but did assure me that he was convinced that he thought I felt perfectly at home in the rainforest.

Brongersma also told me that he was pleased that the biologists had all been on the Antares and in the moss forest. He did say that he thought that the group should have shown better initiative and gone to bivouac 40 earlier. He did not especially name Wim Vervoort, who he had named lead of the biologist group but it was clear that that is who he meant.

Monday the 10th and Tuesday the 11th of August
Base camp. Robbery. Keeping the dance parties secret. Play by Bomdogi.

At the base camp all of the supplies were stored in a barrack which was open and everyone could easily enter. As far as we knew nothing had ever been stolen but now we were not so sure, as the supplies for certain items seemed to be going down really quickly. At first we thought that it was the Moejoe carriers doing the stealing. To find out whether anything was actually being stolen two of our indigenous policemen hid themselves in the warehouse and waited for something to happen. This night it finally did. Towards midnight we were awoken by a loud commotion and a little later the generators were started and the lights went on. It turned out that two Sibillers were trying to steal from the warehouse and had been caught by the police. The police had managed to catch and handcuff one of them. The second person managed to get away. The arrestee had covered himself with pig's fat and was as slippery as an eel. We knew the man because he was in our camp quite often and we knew that he was from Kigonmedib. He was held for a day and after that the police and Jan Sneep (government official) took him back to Kigonmedib. Here, house searches were done and several iron axes and cans of spinach were found. Jan Sneep also had a good talk to them and told them that if they returned all of the stolen supplies the case would be closed. Later the Papuans came to the camp with all kinds of other things that they had previously stolen. Bringing back the tins of spinach was not a problem for them because they had tasted it and said it was too disgusting to eat. They preferred a caterpillar. This event made quite an impression with the Sibillers so we presumed that nothing would be stolen anymore. We were happy that it was not the Moejoe carriers who had stolen anything because we had to work with them for a longer period of time.

In Kigonmedib dance parties were sometimes organised which could last two or three afternoons and evenings at a time. In the morning the women had to work on the gardens which meant they could not party. We could always tell when there was going to be a dance party as we would have a lot of decorated people (especially men) in our camp. They loved having pictures taken of them and demonstrating their dance skills, full of pride. However, they never wanted to tell us when these parties would be taking place. After the robbery we found out why. They had not only stolen canned spinach, but also cans of corned beef which they liked a lot. A highpoint of their parties was to eat the stolen corned beef and any meat left over from pigs. Of course they could not eat the corned beef if people from our camp were there. The kampong Betabib which was close by, was a lot neater than Kigonmedib, and this meant that the people from Betabib looked down on the people from Kigonmedib. The robbery had shown that the people from Betabib really were better than the people from Kigonmedib. Bomdogi, the town elder from Betabib decided to come and demonstrate this the day after the robbery. He came in to the Zilveren Huis, squatted and looked around skittishly and took, with a big smile on his face, something off of the table while he constantly called out something with the word Kigonmedib in it. It seemed that he wanted to show us, with his act, that the thieves from Kigonmedib were bad people.

It was funny to see how there was a rivalry between the two kampongs, somewhat comparable to our Dutch-Belgian rivalry and our Dutch-Belgian jokes. In this aspect there was then not much difference between people from the Stone Age and us.

Wednesday the 12th of August
Dropping of climbing gear.

In order to climb the Juliana peak we needed special climbing gear like warm clothes, tent and sleeping bags. All of this still had to come from Holland. The Twin was broken again, and the Dakota had been asked to drop the supplies that had already arrived in New Guinea. This was possible today because there were not very many clouds. At one point we heard a plane and a bit later we saw it fly over low. After it flew another circle the plane came in low and parallel to our airstrip. Suddenly several bags came falling out of the plane. The plane made another turn, came over again and dropped more bags. Before this drop the reed beds along the Sibil had been mown so as to better find the bags which may also be dropped there. All of the dropped bags were collected by the Papuans and put at a collection spot by the airstrip. Full of pride they brought the bags to the Zilveren Huis. It became something of a competition to see who would be able to collect most of the bags. As far as we could see all of the bags had been found undamaged. It was a very special experience to need equipment in the tropics that reminded me more of a North pole expedition.

Thursday the 13th of August
To the 'bad' kampong Kigonmedib. Offered a cigarette. Pig in the circle. Men made beautiful.

I went to the 'bad' kampong Kigonmedib with my two friends and several other Papuans. This kampong was on the southern slope of the Sibil valley, about an hours walk from the base camp. First we had to wade through the Sibil again. The water from the river was rather low which meant that we did not have to wade much deeper than our knees. The path then gently rose though the rainforest and open places with secondary vegetation where there probably used to be gardens. The path was very muddy and we had to wade through small streams and climb over slippery tree trunks. My friends helped me here as well and held on to me when necessary. After a little less than an hour we arrived in Kigonmedib. In the area of the kampong there were several fenced gardens and parts of secondary vegetation. Sometimes the gardens had small huts built by them. In the gardens I primarily saw sugar cane, sweet potatoes and a lot of weeds. Kigonmedib was slightly higher than our camp and there was a nice view of the Sibil valley from the open areas. De Wilde, Anceaux and Pouwer had spent some time in this kampong for their research and the people were completely used to the 'strange' white people. The kampong looked about the same as Koekding and other kampongs that we had already been and again consisted of a round square with a low fence made of horizontal tree trunks with small family houses on the outside. On the square there were two larger huts, the man house and the men's society. Outside of the fence there were two more huts, one of these was the sacred women's hut. This is where the women stayed when they were on their period or in labour. The mens society was a 'luxurious' house where the roof was partly built from tree trunks instead of only leaves. On the side of the square, a low veranda of tree trunks had been made so that the men could more easily get into the small, square opening. The entrance could also be shut and there several planks ready next to the opening. I was invited by several men to go into their society. This was not easy for me but I was helped to climb in in all kinds of ways by my friends and the head of the kampong. Like in

Betabib, there was not a lot to be seen on the inside. In the middle there was a fireplace made of stones and a smoky fire that a couple of men were sat around. They invited us to sit down too. It was very smoky because of the fire, but also because the men were smoking tobacco. As usual there was no chimney but the smoke disappeared through the roof anyway. There was a lot of talking and joking around and there was a very cosy atmosphere. Sitting in a squat position was not very comfortable for me so it did not take long for me to sit on my knees or stand up, this raised a lot of laughs. They tried to get me to smoke one of the cigarettes which had been rolled by them. This was an awkward moment for me because I do not smoke but I also did not want to offend anyone. I told them in Dutch (which they of course did not understand) and with gestures that I did not smoke. I did not accept the cigarette either which led to more cheerful laughter. I got the impression that they were laughing at the man who offered me the cigarette because he looked a bit sad, but it did not take long before he joined the laughter and talk again. At a certain point I heard some noises behind me and saw that a pig had wandered in. The animal shuffled between us and laid down by the fire. The Papuans hardly reacted to this, it seemed that they were used to the pig being present.

I had seen most of the men before in the base camp. I thought one of them looked rather distinguished. He had a thin stick stuck through his nostril and two sticks in the holes in his nose. He had also put his beard in flat pieces of clay. He had holes in his earlobes and had wrapped these over his ears. For a Papuan he was a very calm person. He spoke a few words of Dutch and from what he said I gathered from what he said that he had often helped Anceaux with creating Sibil-Dutch word lists. Another friendly man had also made himself look very smart. His whole face had been painted red and he had stuck two sticks through his nose. Full of pride he pointed to the button on his nose and around his neck on a piece of wire. He was also the person who almost constantly had a home-made cigarette in his hand. He only put it to his mouth every now and then which meant it often went out and had to be held in the fire to be kept alight.

The women all stayed outside the fenced area and were always stood in groups. They were very curious but mostly kept their distance. It was also noticeable that most of the women and girls had not decorated themselves, unlike the men. They didn't wear any decorations other than the short reed skirts. Only a couple of the women wore string with a shell on it around their neck.

The inhabitants were as usual very friendly and I noticed that they seemed to feel rather ashamed about the theft a couple of days earlier.

Friday the 14th of August
Base camp. To Oemboek with Nijenhuis.

In the morning I went with Nijenhuis to the giant bananas again. He had not been there yet and as he would be leaving the Sibil soon this would be his last chance to see them. After plowing through the rainforest we arrived at the doline and descended. I took a picture of him leaning against a giant banana. From here on we went straight back and we were in time for lunch. Of course Nijenhuis was happy that he had now also seen the giant bananas.

Saturday the 15th of August
Through the dry Sibil to the vanishing point of the river.

It had not rained much for several days. Because of this the Sibil had completely dried out. This was a good opportunity for us to go to the point where the river disappeared into the rocks. I left with my two friends and a couple of others. This time we could walk nearly the whole journey along the dried out riverbed. Here and there, there were some pools that we had to walk around. There was nothing living to be seen in the pools of water. I did often see the stones with an edge covered in the larvae from some kind of insect. An advantage of the dry river bed was of course that I could easily get to the mosses which grew on the crossing zones from above and under water. There was a mass vegetation of *Pseudosymblepharis*, practically without any mixes with other kinds. Close to the vanishing point we could descend somewhat into the ravine via the terraces which we had seen before when the Sibil was a wild river. On most of the terraces there was a hollow caused by the falling water. In some of these there was muller which had only caused it to hollow out more. At the deepest point of the ravine there were three sides surrounded by about 50 metres high, vertical rock walls. We saw a 3-metre-wide hole in which the river disappeared. We could only look down the cave for a couple of metres because it was so dark. It is in this place that Herman Verstappen put food colouring in the water of the river. About 12 kilometres further, by the Songgam, there was a source and people wanted to know whether the river came out here again. A marine went there to keep an eye on the colour of the water and about four hours later the colour did change. Thus it was proven that the source by the Songgam was indeed the Ok Sibil before the river goes into the East-Digoel. I do not know whether the source that I saw by Songgam, a small trickle of water, when I was there with the cadastre group was also part of the Ok Sibil.

Sunday the 16th of August until Monday the 17th of August

Nothing special happened. I dried the previously collected material.

Tuesday the 18th of August
Nijenhuis leaves with Cessna to Tanah Merah.

The Cessna arrived back and took Nijenhuis with it on the journey back to Tanah Merah. Here, Nijenhuis would collect more blood samples.

Wednesday the 19th of August
Shot a pig.

This afternoon two of our carriers entered the camp with a pig they had shot. The kampongs normally had several black pigs, all sows who walked around freely during the day and came home at night and slept with the people by the fire in their houses, as I had also seen in Kigonmedib. The hogs also walked around freely, but remained this way and were allowed to be hunted. The pig was slaughtered, something I did not want to see. The bits of meat were then divided and it tasted very different and a lot nicer to the meat I was used to in Holland.

Thursday the 20th of August
Base camp.

Nothing special happened.

Friday the 21st of August and Saturday the 22nd of August
Fun chaos while drinking coffee. Sent mail. Twin brings fuel.

The staff that served us in the Zilveren Huis had left for Denmatta towards the Juliana peak, so we appointed couple of the local Papuans to help with the housekeeping. These people had never done this kind of work and had probably never seen how everything worked. It was very entertaining to see how they did everything. For the mid-morning coffee, they had made a pot of hot water but they had no idea what to pour it in, so everything was put on the tables, plates, cutlery and even the cheese. After some time, they realised that the coffee needed to go in the mugs. All of this happened during a lot of laughter and discussions. None of this was very hygienic but luckily we did not see everything and the coffee still tasted good. I did not interfere while they were trying to make coffee, I was a lot more interested in how they would solve the problem. After they had received some directions from the others who were also watching them everything went fine. Another time they were asked to wipe down the table. They did not quite know how this was supposed to happen so they threw a pot of coffee over the table and scrubbed it in. Everyone was good humoured and in the days to come they soon figured everything out. This just shows that all things, even the simplest ones, must have been seen at least once.

Sunday the 23rd of August until Tuesday the 25th of August
Material made ready to send. Eating in the Zilveren Huis. Stiring soup. Ghost in the cadastre bivouac. Distorted stamp.

I had gathered that there was a big chance that the biologist group would not be going to Juliana peak and that meant we would be leaving soon, so I decided it was time to get all of the collected material ready to send back to Holland. I got on with drying the material properly, packaging it and labelling it. I had more than enough time to do this so I could do other things in between. I took in everything at the camp one more time and took some more pictures. Most of the expedition members had already left for Tanah Merah or were still in the field. The camp was starting to empty and would soon be deserted.

I heard that Fred van der Weiden was still in bivouac 39A waiting for the clear nights. Knowing him this would not have changed his sense of humour. I did wonder what was happening to keep his group supplied. I did not hear anything about this and I guessed the people there had lost quite a bit of weight.

In the base camp the supplies of food we had slowly became small and monotonous. This was the reason that most of the expedition members went to eat with Jan Sneep from the local governance, where the supplies were more plentiful. I never went for dinner there and always stayed faithful to the Zilveren Huis. I had a good reason for this which I only told people just after we took our leave from the base camp.

A while before I had gone to Jan Sneep's house to have a talk. He was not there but one of our Moejoe carriers was. He was busy making soup in a big pan on the wood fire. He was sat next to the pan on a wooden stool stirring the soup. He was not stirring the soup with a spoon but with his feet. His feet were already rather clean and the dirt was probably in the soup. After this I did not much feel like eating there and kept to the expedition food. I did not tell the others this immediately because I did not want to deny them the lovely soup by Jan Sneep with the special aroma!

One night we were startled by loud noises from the bivouac belonging to the cadastre group. Everyone there was shouting and making as much noise as they could. This lasted for about half an hour after which calm seemed to return The next day, as soon as it was light, the carriers went into the woods behind their bivouac and started shouting and making noises again. The reason for this was that a ghost has been spotted in their bivouac that night which they scared off by making lots of noises. The ghost was later seen in the woods, where it was again scared off with a lot of noise.

The postmark from Jan Sneep's 'post office' were always completely round but a letter that Sneep had stamped for me on the 26th of August was no longer round and had a ding in it. On the 20th of August it was still round from what I could see from a letter stamped on this day. Rumour was that the stamp had flown through the air and had hit something hard. This must have happened between the 20th and 26th of August.

Wednesday the 26th of August
To dance party in Kigonmedib.

During the last couple of days there were often festively dressed men and some women in our camp. Some of the men were painted red and decorated with clay in their hair and beard. One of these men had a long drum with him (called tyfa). He was in a very good mood and demonstrated a dance during which he sung loudly. He has a big bundle of cassowary feathers on his backside which made a grating noise while he walked. Because of these visits we knew that there was a dance party coming in Kigonmedib. These parties usually lasted more than one day and we had heard that today would be the last day where the highpoint would be the killing of a pig. As they no longer had anything that was stolen from us we were allowed to know when it would be. We were invited to come to the party and we went with a group, including Brongersma, during the afternoon. We first had to wade through the Sibil and after this we took the path through the rainforest that we had gone through so many times before. The path was very slippery as usual and full of puddles from the rain the previous days before. From the distance we could hear the singing and drumming from the party. Sadly, I did not bring a camera because I thought it would be too dark to take pictures.

Upon arrival we saw that the party had already started. The men had dressed up festively and their faces were painted with all kinds of shapes in red paint mixed with pig's fat making them shine. Some of them had also painted their upper body, and we also saw people with yellow and black stripes on their foreheads. They had all kinds of jewellery, like a ballpoint, stuck through their nose and ears. On their heads they often had cassowary feathers or birds of paradise feathers, in bundles, attached to their head. Some of them had big bunches of these feathers on their backsides. They also had the stomach bands which were used to stick more decoration in, as well as in their arm and leg bands. The finishing touch was the brightly painted penis shafts.

The women had also painted themselves festively in all kinds of patterns, though often to a lesser extent than the men. The women were not allowed to use the red pig fat and their red colour was duller than the men. They often wore a necklace with one or more mussel shells on it, and sometimes with pigs teeth or other things. They also wore birds of paradise feathers in bundles on their head and over their short reed skirts they wore a bundle of longer reed stems, over their backside which also made a grating sound.

After we had watched them for a while we heard the singing and drumming getting louder in the distance. That were the inhabitants of kampong Ebonanterawho were there to celebrate the party with the people from Kigonmedib. When they came closer they announced their arrival with a high-pitched and quick 'oewa-oewa' call which was answered by the people from Kigonmedib. We had heard this call often when a group of Papuans neared a different kampong. The group consisted of women who were surrounded by men who were shouting loudly and drumming on their tyfa's. Some of the men had brought their bow and arrows with which they kept pretending to shoot. Upon arrival to the kampong the men climbed over the fence to the central square, the women also did this but in a different place to the men. The newcomers were also painted and dressed up in all kinds of ways. We stayed to the side together with most of the children, awaiting what was going to happen.

The women took each other arm in arm and formed themselves like a fan and moved like this, whilst singing, over the muddy square during which they rhythmically dropped through their knees. During this movement the bundles of reeds attached to their back sides made a scraping noise. The men walked one behind each other, also singing, and sinking through their knees. They then stood still close to the men's house and then repeated the circle. When someone got tired, someone else would take over. This could go on for hours on end without any variation.

At the end of the party a couple of pigs were always slaughtered. A fire was then made on which the meat was roasted that would later be divided among everyone. We did not witness the end or the slaughtering because we wanted to get back through the forest while there was still enough light left to see. On the way back we had a couple of small boys as guides who led us back to our camp without any issues. During this journey I heard Brongersma mutter that wading through mud and over tree trunks in the half dark was not his favourite past time. I completely agreed with this but for me it was the first (and only) time that I did not enjoy walking through the rainforest. Luckily, it did not take long before we saw the silver ribbon of the Sibil river. Thanks to our guides who warned us about all of the obstacles we made it to the river without falling over too many times. After wading through this the base camp was quickly in sight. Here we were welcomed, like every night, by hundreds of flying fire flies. We could hear the singing and drumming of the party until deep in the night and we fell asleep to this noise feeling content.

Thursday the 27th of August
Peace offering from Kigonmedib.

Throughout the morning a couple of Papuans, including the thief from Kigonmedib came to the camp with two pigs feet. These feet were meant to make up for the theft. With this the whole affair was dealt with to everyone's satisfaction.

It seemed likely that we would be leaving the Sibil via Merauke and Tanah Merah to Hollandia.

Friday the 28th of August
Definitely not going to the Juliana peak.

Not long ago Brongersma had asked me and the other biologists whether we would like to go to the Juliana Mountains. We would then go with the geologist group to Denmatta at the foot of the Juliana Mountains, a journey of three days. From there the real journey would begin. Of course, I was looking forward to this, but only up to the snow boundary as higher than this there would be nothing for me to collect. Eventually Brongersma decided that it would not be responsible to send the biologist and geologist group to the Juliana Mountains because the supply of food could not be guaranteed. The supply of petrol was not sufficient and the supply by the Twin from Hollandia was suspended due to the heavy cloud cover. To do everything by carrier was not practical either because, we not only needed food, but also a dry-oven and a lot of collection and packaging material in order to do the research. Brongersma eventually decided to only allow the geologists to go to the Juliana Mountains. I thought this was a great shame, but I did understand Brongersma's decision.

Saturday the 29th of August until Monday the 31st of August
Base camp. Making everything ready to leave.

Nothing special happened in these days. We were waiting for the Twin to take us to Sentani. Now the plan was no longer that we would fly through Tanah Merah and Merauke to Sentani, but instead we would fly the Twin straight to Sentani.

Tuesday the 1st of September
French-Dutch film expedition by Gaisseau an hour in the Sibil.

In the start of the afternoon the Twin arrived with the French-Dutch film expedition, belonging to Gaisseau in the base camp. They made a landing in Sibil on the way to Asmat to film there. During the landing we saw that the door had been taken off and cameras had been installed that were filming the landing. A big group of people came out of the plane who went with Brongersma and the rest of the welcoming committee to the Zilveren Huis. After some time the pilot came back out and looked up at the sky with a worried face, as usual the clouds were closing in. If the Twin still wanted to leave today it would have to be fast. The group came out of the Zilveren Huis soon after and got in the Twin which quickly took off. Just in time we saw the plane leave through a small hole in the clouds in the direction of Tanah Merah.

Wednesday the 2nd of September
Saying goodbye to the Sibil.

There was a good chance that the Twin could take us to Sentani the next day, so I walked through the whole of the camp and the surrounding area in order to take everything in one last time. I also took the time to say goodbye to the people who would not be joining us to Sentani such as, Jan Sneep, Brongersma, and Venema. In the research barrack there was a map of Dutch New Guinea in which the ridges were clearly visible. I thought it was a nice map and because we had spent such a long time looking at it I liked the idea of taking it with me as a memento. No one else seemed interested so I took the map off of the wall and took it with me.

I felt quite melancholic about my leave from the Sibil because I realised that I would probably not be coming back. I would see the other expedition members in Holland again, but my two Papuan friends that I had had so many adventures with, I would never see again and I found this the hardest.

Thursday the 3rd of September[11]
Departure by Twin from the Sibil to Sentani.

As there had not been a lot of rain in the last couple of days the Twin arrived at the agreed upon time to take us to Sentani. The group was made up of the biologists (Van Heijningen, Kalkman, Staats, and me), Anceaux, Reynders and De Wilde. Vervoort would not be joining because he had left for Tanah Merah earlier to make arrangements regarding the postage of the collected materials. Brongersma had arranged that we could stay with several individuals (for a small fee from the expedition) while waiting for further transport to Sentani and Holland. The biologist group could stay with Dr. Romeijn, who took us to his house in Ifar after our arrival in Sentani.

Friday the 4th of September until Saturday the 12th of September
Ifar. McArthurs monument. Waterfall. Tree-kangaroo. Van der Weiden in Kloof camp. Paid for nothing myself.

Ifar was a small place at the foot of the Cycloop Mountains. During the end phases of the Second World War several hangars had been placed

---

[11] I am not completely sure that we left the Sibil on the third of September, it could also have been the fourth.

here after the invasion of the Americans. Dr. Romeijn lived in one of these. The hangars had been made very cosy with flowers, especially *Hibiscus*. There were several big tiger spiders in the area waiting for their prey.

Ifar was at about 300 metres above sea level, and it was somewhat cooler than in Hollandia. Dr. Romeijn's servant had washed and ironed all of our clothes so that they looked all neat and tidy again. Of course I looked in the neighbourhood for mosses but I could not find anything. We spent the whole time in Ifar talking about our experiences, writing letters, and doing nothing. We did make a trip to the General McArthur monument. This is a memorial stone on a plinth. It had been established by the Americans just after the expulsion of the Japanese by the Americans as commanded by General McArthur.

The most interesting trip that we still made (on the 7th of September) was to a waterfall on the edge of the forest on the foothills of the Cycloon Mountains. The waterfall could easily be reached by foot. The first part went through secondary bushes that slowly changed into secondary forest. At the foot of the waterfall there was a pool where we could swim in the clear water. The rocks by the water were full of lizards, and I was able to collect some more mosses in this area.

We were told that the tree-kangaroo that we had seen in bivouac 39 had been taken to Hollandia and temporarily put in an area where furniture had been stored before. This furniture had been treated with DDT that was still on the floor and the tree-kangaroo got too much of this in his system. Eventually it had killed him.

We were also informed that Van der Weiden had left bivouac 39A towards the end of August, but he had managed to do his measurements. His patience was eventually rewarded and because of that we now know the exact coordinates of bivouac 39A on the Antares.

After the Antares, Van der Weiden went to the Kloof camp. He had promised me, if he got the opportunity, he would collect some mosses for me on his was to Tanah Merah. From the Kloof camp he went with a group by pirogue down the East-Digoel. On the way the pirogue toppled a couple of times but eventually everyone arrived safely in Kawakit.[12]

During my first leave from the base camp to the sick post in Hollandia-Binnen (4th of May) I had got some money from Brongersma but I hardly had to use it. Everywhere I went I did not have to pay. All of the bills were sent straight to the Expedition. This happened for the hotel in Hollandia-Binnen, the sick post, the barrack in Tanah Merah (accommodation and meals), boat and plane trips. It was only at the post office, the Chinese restaurant and the Chinese toko in Hollandia-Binnen where I had to use his money.

Sunday the 13th of September
Flight from Sentani to Biak.

Leaving from Sentani to Biak was planned for this day. Dr. Romeijn drove us to the airport Sentani, which was situated nearby. I had no reservations for the flight from Biak to Sydney so I was not sure whether I would be able to continue on to Sydney the next day. Once we arrived at Sentani we telegraphed KLM to ask if there would be a place for me on the KLM-flight from Biak to Sydney. After some time the message came from Biak that I would be able to continue my flights. This meant that I really would leave Sentani with the Twin to Biak and the usual ceremony of checking in and weighing my baggage could start. From the departure hall we saw the Twin that I would fly to Biak with. I saw a man get out of the plane with a painted war shield that was bigger than he was.

After saying our goodbyes to Dr. Romeijn and the biologists, who could only leave for Holland later, I got into the plane which quickly left for Biak. I saw the Sentani lake under me again, but quickly the view was

---

12 To my surprise when I had been back in Holland for a while I got a package from New Guinea with mosses that had been collected by him in the Kloof camp. They were all in good state and it seemed that they had survived the pirogue quite well.

impeded by the clouds. After some time we landed at airport Mokmer on Biak where our journey had started half a year ago. Because I was a member of the expedition I was offered free shelter by the Marines. In the afternoon I had time to look around the area. Hardly anything had changed in the area, or in the restaurant since our last visit. The Papuan attendants were still wearing bright white shirts and they were just as friendly as they had been previously.

Monday the 14th of September
Flight from Biak to Sydney.

After half a year a definite end had come to the adventure in New Guinea and a new adventure was awaiting me in New Zealand. During the flight over New Guinea we could hardly see the landscape because our plane was flying too high to clearly see. When we neared Australia the clouds had disappeared and the coast was clearly visible. It was already close to evening and the desert below us was a bright red. This lasted for quite a while, until it became too dark to see anything. After several hours Sydney came into view with its sea of lights. Straight after this we started our descent and we landed at the airport in Sydney. After the customs inspection I was driven to a hotel in the centre of Sydney.

Tuesday the 15th of September
Sydney.

As I would not be leaving for New Zealand until the next day I had the whole day to look around the town. My hotel was close to the famous Harbour Bridge, which was a good starting point to explore the rest of the town. Practically under the bridge there were some small shops. One of them was a music shop with sheet music where they even had several pieces of classical music. The centre was nearby with tall skyscrapers and busy traffic which felt rather oppressive so I did not spend much time there. On top of this I did not really like walking around by myself so it did not take long before I went back to my hotel. There were a lot of taxi's criss-crossing through the city. None of the cars used indicators but instead the drivers signalled with their hands through the open windows. The traffic drove on the left and it was funny to see how, if a car wanted to turn right the drivers waved their right hand up and to the left over the roof.

Towards the evening I went the hotel restaurant and sat at one of the many empty tables as you were used to doing in Europe. This, however, was not the done thing and I was directed to a table where an elderly couple was already sat and who spoke English. On top of this the staff did not think my clothes were neat enough because I was not wearing a tie, they even offered to lend me one. In my opinion they were overreacting, my khaki coloured jeans and shirt had been washed and ironed in Ifar. This is when I had a cheeky idea, and I told them that my clothes were the summer uniform from the Dutch marines on New Guinea. Apparently they believed this and suddenly I was dressed well enough to stay in the dining room.

Wednesday the 16th of September
Flight from Sydney to Wellington (New Zealand).

After breakfast in the hotel I took the taxi to the airport. I had asked the receptionist if they could call a taxi for me but it did not work like that. Someone went to the exit of the hotel and waved his hand, and almost directly there was a taxi waiting. My plane to Wellington left in the afternoon so I had a long wait at the airport. In the plane I was sat next to a New Zealander that I got talking to. He asked me where I had come from and where I was going. I told him that I had just come back from an expedition to the unknown areas of the Central Mountains of Dutch New Guinea. He seemed to think this was interesting and upon arrival at Wellington he told a reporter who came and interviewed me. He took a picture of me with a very old fashioned camera. He asked me all kinds of things about my vision of Dutch New Guinea and what should happen about it. I presume that he worked for a newspaper but I never saw the photo or the article. After this I went to the hotel that I had had reserved in Australia. During the evening meal, to my surprise, someone made a comment about the fact I was not wearing a tie.

Thursday the 17th of September
Flight from Wellington to Napier. Arrival in Taradale.

In the morning, to my surprise, there was an early knock on the door and a friendly woman came in with a tray of tea. After this I went to the dining room where they served bacon and eggs for breakfast. The bacon was dripping with fat so I decided to keep to the eggs. After this I took a taxi to the airport for the flight to Napier. Upon arrival I saw my brother, Gerrit (now Gerald) for the first time in more than ten years. My mother, who had taken the boat to New Zealand was also there, as was Valery, my brother's wife, and their daughter Fiona. My brother brought us to his house in Taradale, close to Napier. This was rather an emotional experience after all of the adventures and the long-time apart.

A whole new period in my life was about to start.

Tuesday the 22nd of September
Asked about my opinion.

I was visited by a reporter from the Hawke's Bay Herald Tribune. It seemed that the reporter I had met at the airport in Wellington had passed my brothers address in Taradale on. The matter of Dutch New Guinea was very much in the news in this period and he asked me what my opinion was about the possible transfer of Dutch New Guinea to Indonesia. I told him that I would prefer to see Dutch New Guinea become part of Papua New Guinea in time, but that this would not happen because Indonesia wanted the area. It was either stay and wage war with Indonesia, or give them the area. This did not make a choice very hard...

Personal relationships with other expedition members and inhabitants of the base camp

During the whole of the expedition I did not run in to any issues with other members of the expedition, except for my disagreement with Wim Vervoort in bivouac 39A on the Antares. It was easy to have a good talk with Brongersma, the scientific leader of the expedition. With chief Venema, the technical leader of the expedition it was harder for me to gain contact. He was also not very loved by the other members of the expedition. The diminishing supplies at the start of the expedition were fairly or unfairly blamed on him. In all practicality it came down to the fact that I never had a real conversation with him. The same can be said about lieutenant Nicolas. We did not have much to do with the other marines that were in our camp but what little contact we did have was good. One exception was Corporal Bril who I, and others, often talked with. He was always very helpful and cheerful and I can remember the nice bread he used to make if there was flour available and the cheerful harmonica tunes he woke us with whilst on the Antares. I also got along excellently with the Marine Ferry Brandenburg who I mostly got to know on the Antares. The same can be said for the marines that I shared a room with while in Tanah Merah. I did not have much contact with the people from the cadastre group, other than, of course, Fred van der Weiden who I liked a lot. During and before our trek to the Sibil and also later in bivouac 39A I learnt a lot from him about walking through the rainforest, but especially about patience. I only saw the geologists Bär, Cortel, Escher, and Verstappen very little as they were almost always in the field. I only met Bär duing his leave for the trek to Hollandia and the others mostly upon their return from the top of the Antares in bivouac 39 and 39A. I was however very aware that we were only able to climb the Antares because of their hard work. They created the road from the foot of the mountain to the top so that the biologists could also get up.

I got along very well with Jaap Reynders as well as André de Wilde, both collected several mosses for me from areas where I was not going. Of course I noticed that there was some friction between André de Wilde and Brongersma, but on a personal level the relationships were still good. I got also got along very well with Pouwer and Anceaux, though the latter was rather tiring as he talked a lot. Although Nijenhuis was only in the Sibil for a short amount of time I got along well with him as well. Naturally most of my time was spent with the biologist group because we did a lot of the same things. I felt most comfortable with Cees van Heijningen, John Staats and Herman Verstappen. The relationship with Cees Kalkman was also good but somewhat more distanced. It was only with Wim Vervoort that I sometimes felt uncomfortable. Whether that was because of the 'borrowed rope', what happened in bivouac 39A, or that we just did not work together I do not know. He most likely thought that I was just as distanced as I thought he was. In the Sibil there were also the government officials Jan Sneep, Dasselaar, and Herberts who were not officially part of the expedition but were still liked by everyone. The latter two were only present at the start of our expedition. The last two members arrived later and were the two journalists, Van Sprang and Klaarenbeek. Van Sprang was not really liked by anyone. Klaarenbeek however was a friendly and nice person who everyone could get along with.

Jan Sneep was a government official in the Sibil Valley during the expedition period. Though he was not officially a member of the expedition we did have a lot of contact with him and the expedition had a lot to thank him for. He solved the conflict with the kampong about the theft from our supply barrack in a way that was acceptable for everyone. When, towards the end of the expedition food supplies were very low most of the expedition members ate with Jan Sneep because he still had enough supplies. He was always very helpful and everyone could get along with him.

We had little contact with the people in charge of the helicopters. An exception however was Willem Warman, the leader of the pilots. I had good talks with him several times, I had noticed however that the relationship between Brongersma and Willem was not very good.

Brongersma thought that the pilots were not motivated to fly to the base camp as soon as possible. Brongersma blamed the fact that the expedition had a bad start because of the supply issues on the lack of motivation from the pilots. Brongersma seriously considered moving the whole of the base camp to Katem (as can be seen from his diary entry). From here a path would be cut via the valley of the Ok Iwoer to the foot of the Antares. This became Bär's job.

The chopping down of the trees to create a path went slowly because the team doing it could not receive their supplies via helicopter. Because of this the plan to move the base camp was deserted. I was very happy about this as there was nothing for me to do there.

After a serious talk between Brongersma and Warman it was eventually worked out that the helicopters could get to the base camp and the supplying of several other bivouacs could start.

Fred van der Weide who had nothing to do with any of this, did not trust the helicopters very much. Instead he took a hundred carriers from the Moejoe area to ensure that there would be supplies. It is with this group that I walked back from Tanah Merah to the base camp.

Chance Meetings

After this experience I had several chance meetings with other members of the expedition, as you will read below they really were rather coincidental.

Andre de Wilde was appointed Professor by Special Appointment of cultural anthropology in Groningen. He then moved to Haren, and bought the 'Zonnehof' house where I used to study Zoology. Coincidentally, it turned out that his daughter did the same study as my daughter, Marieke, and that they knew each other. This caused us to regain contact with each other once we found out.

Jaap Reynders lived in Eext where he had bought a small farm with his wife. I went to the area to speak at the 'KNNV' (Royal Dutch Natural History Society) about mosses in general. It turned out that Jaap was one of the people in the audience. I recognised him immediately and he acted like he did not recognise me. Later he admitted that this was not the case and that he knew exactly who I was. Up until his death in 2009 we frequently got together and became rather good friends.

Jan Sneep though not officially part of our expedition also became part of my life after the expedition through our wives. His wife was a keen potter as was my wife. They had a caravan close to Meppel (Ufferde) where Petra van Heesbeen also lived. Petra was a good friend of my wife and taught pottery workshops that Jan's wife ended up going to. They got talking about the strange jobs some people had, and used the example of a man who spends all his life working with mosses and manages to earn a living with it. When Sneep's wife told Sneep about this, he said that Petra must have been talking about me. Petra knew about my love of mosses through my wife and through this strange connection Jan Sneep and I were able to get back in touch with each other.

Though I did see the other members at reunions of the expedition they did not become part of my daily life and the contact was infrequent.

Epilogue

The expedition was a great success for me. For starters the base camp was in an ideal location with varied terrain. This meant that there was great diversity of plants and mosses at hands reach. The choice of location of bivouac 39A was also very successful because of the rich collection of mosses, other plants and especially orchids. The fact that I did not have the right equipment to collect, dry, and package what I collected was not such a big problem as I had ample opportunity to collect in the area of the base camp at a later time. I was also very lucky to injure myself at the start of our expedition whilst still in the base camp which meant I had to go back to Hollandia to treat the wound in the polyclinic in Hollandia-Binnen. After this healed I went to Tanah Merah where I had ample opportunity to collect from the lowland rainforest area. My luck continued as Van der Weiden came to Tanah Merah to charter a great number of carriers that the cadastre group would need in the Sibil Valley and Antares area. I was able to join this group which gave me the opportunity to collect mosses at different heights during the 14-day trip (from 100 metres to 1300 metres). For me, this journey was one of the highlights of the whole expedition. Upon arrival in the Sibil the Antares project was just about to start which meant my timing was spot on. The climbing of the Antares was a big experience and literally and figuratively the highlight of the expedition. The idea that we were the first people to climb the West top of the mountain was very special. During this climb I was able to collect material from different heights, which meant I was left with a good impression of the moss vegetation between 1300 and 1380 metres. As strange as it may seem, the crashing of one of our helicopters I personally found to my advantage as it meant we had to walk back to the Sibil instead of fly. This meant I was able to collect in even more areas. I was very pleased with regards to the harvest of mosses during the whole of the expedition, even with the difficulties at the start of the expedition. The only thing I thought was a shame is that the biologists were unable to take part in the exploration of the Juliana Mountains. In my opinion the scientific results of the expedition would have been more interesting if more attention had been paid to the climbing of the Juliana Mountains instead of the focus on the trek to Hollandia by the geologists. For me personally meeting the people who still live in the Stone Age was also a highlight. I now have a completely different view of these people and I grew to care for them very much, they have a special place in my heart.

All of the collected plants went straight to the Rijksherbarium (States herbarium) in Leiden. Of the mosses duplicates were sent for testing to Groningen and several other herbariums. A total of 324 different kinds of mosses were collected of which about 50 taxa (species, family, or class) were described as new to science (Zanten 1964). From these new taxa about 30% was withdrawn (often because the variation width of existing kinds was larger than first thought) and another 30% received a lower level (mostly as subspecies or variety of an existing species). There is still 30% which is seen as new to science. All new taxa of the mosses were described based on the material present in herbarium GRONINGANUM. The holotypes are in herb GRO. The types in herbarium L and other herbarium are isotypes copies of these isotypes were sent to herbariums all over the world. The lichens and liverworts are being or have been processed by several specialists, the outcome of this is unknown to me.

Consulted literature

Brandenburg van den Gronden, F. 2012. *Bivak Frigidaire* (een oog-getuige verslag van het helicopter ongeluk): pp. 141-155. *We missen één man, zestien eigenzinnige verhalen van veteranen.*

Brongersma, L.D. 1959. Dagboek. Ongepubliceerde Rapporten.

Brongersma, L.D. & G.F. Venema 1960. *Het Witte Hart van Nieuw-Guinea*, 281 + 11 pp. Scheltens & Giltay, Amsterdam.

Kalkman, C. 1963. *Description of vegetation types in the Star Mountains Region, West New Guinea.* – Nova Guinea 15, Botany: 247-261 + Plate XVII-XXI.

Sneep, J. 2005. *Einde van het stenen tijdperk* – 181 pp. Rozenberg, Amsterdam.

Verstappen, H.Th. 2006. *Een bezoek aan de steentijd: het sterren gebergte*: 115-127 – *In zwerftocht door een wereld in beweging.* 164 pp. Van Gorcum, Assen.

Zanten, B.O. van 1964. *Mosses of the Star Mountains Expedition.* – Nova Guinea 16, Botany: 263-368 + Plate XXII-XXXVI.

Zanten, B.O. van 2003. *Verspreiding en evolutiesnelheid bij mossen – In kaart gebracht met kapmes en kompas met het Koninklijk Nederlands Aardrijkskundig Genootschap op expeditie tussen 1873 en 1960*: p. 108-110. ABP/KNAG (A. Wentholt, red.)

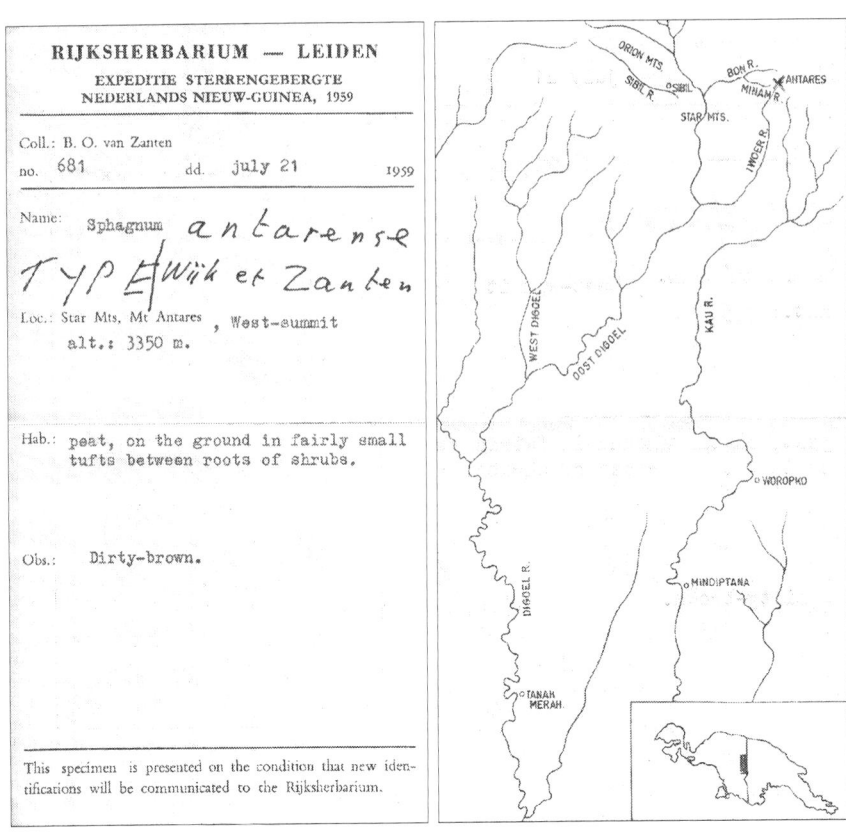

To the left an example of a herbarium label. These were filled in based on my notebooks. Upon return to the Netherlands all of me collected mosses were given such labels. To the right the back of the label in which the area of discovery of the individual moss was marked.

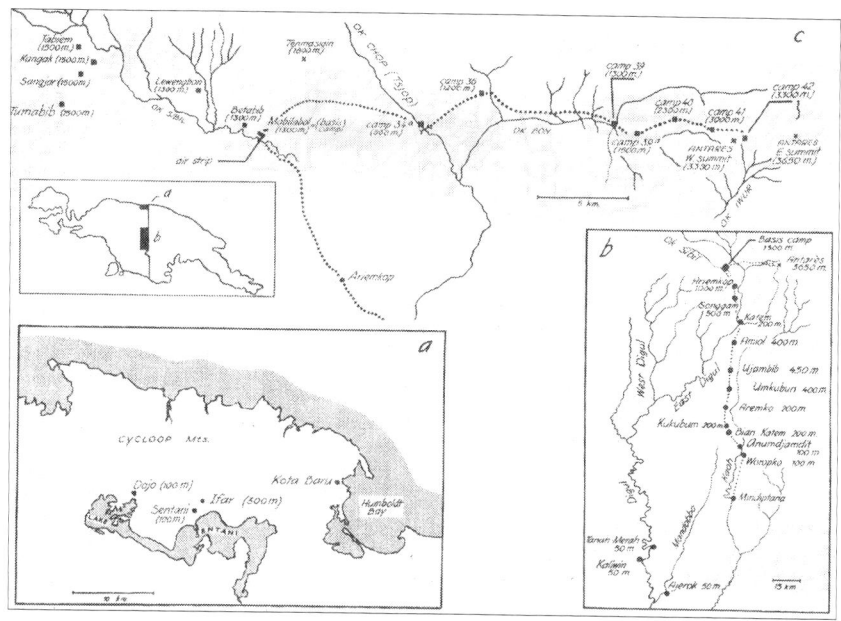

An overview of Dutch New Guinea in which the location
of certain places is indicated.

The crest of the Antares Mountains with the West top (3480 m), as seen from the North-West and the East top (3650 m), the highest top of the Antares.

For more pictures from the expedition please visit:
www.bovanzanten.nl

Printed in Great Britain
by Amazon